Living WITH AN UGLY WOMAN

Living WITH AN UGLY WOMAN

God's Pathway
THROUGH THE PROCESS
TO A POSITION OF PROMISE

SANDI BURRIS

outskirtspress
DENVER, COLORADO

You make contact the author at:

sandiburrisministries@hotmail.com or sandiburrisministries@gmail.com

Sandi Burris Ministries
P.O. Box 444
Malvern, AR 72104

Contents

PART 1:

UGLY BEFORE IT GETS UGLY

CHAPTER 1

Moving Past A Bad Past

FOR GENERATIONS JACOB has given preachers, filled with fiery passion and a holy hatred for sin sizzling sermons to convict and compel the most atrocious sinners to acknowledge their demoralized lifestyles. Envisioning the fires of hell lapping at their back, the hearers sit white-knuckled as they simmer in their sinful desires. The conviction is so strong they, like Jacob, begin to evaluate. It is a sad scenario as they recognize their need but are unwilling to surrender. As they hear these heaven sent messages, hearts smitten and knees buckled under them, they enter into a wrestling match with God.

Sweating, spitting screaming and with snorting nostrils flared, preachers have railed on and on about Jacob's low estate. For eons, he has provided food for thought for many Sunday morning congregations. Jacob has been verbally skinned, boiled, broiled, baked and plated. Dished up for the backsliding to chew on, each preacher convinced his manna preparation of Jacob's unholy existence will provide the balanced menu required to bring health and wholeness to the total man, if ingested.

With high hopes of conversion for the lost and undone, preachers have long used Jacob as an example of everything you never aspire to do or be. Could it be these fist pounding, fire breathing, sin slaying men and women of God have missed a great lesson in Jacob's story?

Should they have prepared a more thorough investigation, avoiding a rush to judgment? The result of their preformed opinion is a narrative of degradation rather than an account of a covenant son who through a process found his way.

I do not want to be presumptuous but I carry a slightly different opinion of Jacob and the details of his life. As one of my favorite Bible characters, Jacob has been a source of strength to my faith. His story intensified my confidence in a covenant keeping God. It helps me when I study characters of the Bible whose lives appear less than promising. Their stories inspire hope for both myself and those who directly affect my life and appear somewhat unseemly. Jacob must have had his reasons for his erratic, sometimes deceptive, self-serving behavior but none of that influenced God to withdraw the covenant plan for Jacob's life.

Jacob's life and the fulfillment of the covenant promise of God that blanketed him were all about the process.

What is process? Process is a natural or in this case supernatural phenomenon marked by gradual changes leading toward a particular result. The word process is without a particularly negative connotation but definitely does not carry an altogether positive tone. When you hear someone say, I am trying to process, or you must go through the process sighs and groans are likely to rise. The notion of going through a mandatory process to reach a designated end denotes time devoted, effort exerted and the expectation of challenging experiences along the way. Each individual situation is different and the amount of time, toil or trouble required to make it where you desire to be is specific.

A huge problem for most of us is our patience for and understanding of the process God has designed for our life in order to fulfill His promise to us and through us is in short supply. We want what we want when we want it and we think we know exactly how to get from A to Z.

In addition, we believe God should reveal the entire outline for His plan and promise for our lives. This is yet another hindrance to promise fulfillment.

We have less appreciation for those things handed to us without earning them. When we have invested ourselves fully....struggled, worked with, suffered for something we desire, we carry a greater appreciation for it. Realizing in the end the process by which we attained the desire is something we've grown to embrace.

Jacob, son of Isaac, grandson of Abraham is a beautiful example of promise meets process. He and his motley crew are a flawed family carrying a precious covenant promise without a detailed map of where to go or how to get there. Though there was no step-by-step plan laid out for Jacob, his predecessors or his successors, if we look back at his life from our perspective maps out an intricate plan for us regarding the process necessary to fulfill the promise of God for our lives.

One way for us to truly grasp how God can and will bring His promise to fulfillment regardless of circumstance, is to follow Jacob through his process very closely. The promise of God rests on Jacob and his entire family. His willingness to embrace that promise is evident but the realities of Jacob's life loom ever present. Whatever the vantage point you choose when examining Jacob's situation, the process he had to go through was plain, even prominent. Not only that, at times, it was downright ugly. Jacob began with an ugly past and just when he thinks he will escape the ugly and seize the beautiful, sweet reward of promise, he finds himself smack in the middle of something even uglier!

AN UGLY PAST BUT GOD BRINGS HIM THROUGH

We all have those, generally family, who play a significant role in shaping us into the people we become. Jacob had such a family.

Great importance was placed on family in biblical times. Tremendous significance was placed on the advice passed down from grandfathers and fathers. Strong admonition was given to sons who carried on after the father had passed. To understand Jacob, we must understand where he came from.

The story did not begin with Jacob. The promise did not begin with Jacob and most certainly, the process did not begin with Jacob. God's plan was in action long before Jacob came on the scene. In order to understand him better, we will explore those who had significance in his life and influence on him as a man of God.

JACOB'S MOTHER REBEKAH

Likely the most significant in Jacob's life was his mother, Rebekah. Investigating Rebekah, we find she was somewhat of a free-spirit. Examining her younger years we are drawn to a man named Eleazar, Abrahams's servant, who is sent to search for a wife for Isaac, the young promised son of Abraham. As a posse sent to find Isaac a wife arrives at her father's home, Rebekah, showing no apprehension waters the camels of the group of men she does not know. When presented with the suggestion of marriage to Isaac, a man she has never seen before and the chance to live in a place she has never been before, she readily agrees to go with them. Without hesitation, Rebekah agrees to become Isaac's wife. She eagerly embraces the opportunity to leave the familiarity of friends and family to explore the unfamiliar.

Seemingly unafraid of where her impetuous decision might take her, Rebekah showed she was anything but a shy and reserved young lady. The open horizon that lay ahead was stimulating to her sense of adventure and seemed an excellent opportunity for a young woman desiring new experiences and excitement not available to her at home. Rebekah's distinctive personality traits would later prove to uncover a slight flaw in her character as well. Her innovative, take no prisoners attitude would manifest itself in one of her offspring and completely change the course of his future.

JACOB'S FATHER ISAAC

Isaac, Jacob's father was the promised and long-awaited son of Abraham and Sarah. Isaac's nature was exactly the opposite of this free-spirited wife Rebekah. He was quiet and passive in nature.

Remember Isaac? He was the young man of our Bible stories who, at a mature age laid down at his father's instruction and allowed Abraham to draw a knife on him with the intent to kill him. Now *that* is laid back!

Lackadaisical, laissez-faire and possibly a bit apathetic, Isaac must have admired the fearless, energetic temperament of beautiful Rebekah. She was everything he was not. Her ability to forge ahead into whatever she fancied must have intrigued Isaac.

REBEKAH'S BARRENNESS

For years, Rebekah bore no children, regardless of the covenant hovering over this covenant couple. Did this surprise them? Maybe, but it shouldn't have, it was a familiar scenario.

Isaac himself came along after his mother had suffered many years of barrenness. Through firsthand knowledge of that experience, Isaac certainly knew what NOT to do. After experiencing the family drama of Hagar and Isaac's half-brother Ishmael's dramatic exit from the family, Isaac did not want to make the same mistake.

Therefore, Isaac prayed to the Lord on behalf of his wife. Some even say, he prayed WITH his wife because she was barren.

Barrenness was considered a curse and this family of promise was no stranger to that curse. It ran vehemently through these early generations of God's covenant people. God's promise to His people from the beginning was that of innumerable descendants, yet the women struggled to bear children time and again. The irony is unmistakable. God's absolute power is undeniable.

Sometimes our God given promise seems directly connected to or contingent upon our overcoming insurmountable odds and obstacles in our background, family history or personality. If the strength of our promise is financial blessing, a spirit of poverty endeavors to reign over our finances. If promise is of affecting the lives of others through communication, we find ourselves in a spiritual battle over our speaking ability. If our promise is of many children, barrenness may boldly present itself.

In a way, it is as though a lack of productivity attempts to gain the upper hand in whatever area we possess promise. Make no mistake; this does not stop God but it does threaten to stop us.

As with all obstacles, God allows certain situations for His glory. If God gave you a promise of prosperity and your natural ability through your occupation provided wealth to what would you likely attribute your prosperity? Self? Your own ability? If God gives you a promise of prosperity and it comes to you through no innate ability or apparent achievement of your own and only through a God-guided process, then who gets the credit? That's right, God.

Time is always an issue as well when dealing with promise. When God gives us a promise, we are as excited as children awaiting a coveted birthday gift. The anticipation is almost unbearable! Rarely is the manifestation of our promise as predictable in timing as a birthday gift. Rarely does it manifest in the way we expect.

ISAAC PRAYED FOR REBEKAH TO CONCEIVE

God's covenant with Abraham passed on to Isaac was of descendants you could not number and prosperity you would not believe. Yet, Isaac and Rebekah had waited twenty years to conceive. Not only was this a long time to wait for the promise of God to manifest, it was a long time to carry this curse of barrenness.

Father and son shared the same promise and Isaac was well aware that he too was a long time coming. He knew to be patient and allow God time to move. Still, the couple must have been anxious. The difference is that Isaac saw benefit in entreating the Lord for Rebekah's conception rather than attempting to make it happen through another avenue. This would prove to be a wise choice.

You wonder as Isaac prayed for Rebekah to conceive, whether he had any idea what he was truly asking for. Many times we hear people say, "be careful what you pray for" and so we should. Isaac and Rebekah should have as well. For someone who preferred the laid back and unpretentious, the family Isaac was about to acquire would be anything but ordinary.

Rebekah finally conceived and the excitement was immeasurable. *Would it be a son? What would his personality be?* Her excitement soon turned to concern as the movement inside her body seemed out of the ordinary. Her questions were likely numerous. After all, she had never been pregnant before. The hope and expectation of an uneventful pregnancy was quickly laid to rest. *Was it supposed to feel like this? I knew there'd be movement but this seems much too much!*

Surely she had discussions about the process with other women and had some idea of what to expect. There were beautiful, joyous signs of life but also a bit of concern.

Rebekah was unaware that this movement was a physical manifestation of the future spiritual turmoil and power struggle that would befall her family. At this time she simply wanted to know what was going on with the baby inside her body. In the days without ultra-sound or sonogram, Rebekah could only speculate.

Genesis 25:22 says the babies jostled each other within her. She couldn't help but wonder, *what is happening to me?* Rebekah was experiencing struggle within but did not know the true cause. She knew the activity in her womb was out of the ordinary and thankfully she knew what to do when facing out of the ordinary situations. She went to God.

As Christians, we too are covenant people, promise carriers and also struggle to understand what goes on in our daily lives. It seems an immense struggle often to the point of discouragement especially since we truly desire to do it God's way. We want to find the correct answer, the right way, not just blindly submit to a sinful nature in a sin-filled world.

Rebekah knew to seek God if she wanted to find an answer. Like Rebekah, when we run upon extreme circumstances, we have no alternative. We must inquire of God if we want answers. It is imperative, some might say a no-brainer to go to the one whose plan it is. Until we do, we have no hope of understanding God's purpose for some of the unpleasant, perplexing and even tragic experiences.

As Rebekah sought the Lord regarding her situation, God did speak but my guess is it was unlike anything she expected to hear.

TWO NATIONS IN REBEKAH'S WOMB

The Lord told Rebekah she was carrying two nations in her womb. She was the mother of two peoples. These two peoples would eventually be separated and one would be much stronger than the other but there was a twist. The older would serve the younger.

I am sure this perplexed Rebekah. How could something so out of the ordinary be God's will? It was widely understood the younger siblings would serve the eldest. Still, Rebekah was a woman who went to a strange land and married a man she'd never seen without reservation, so she likely did not pause long before accepting and embracing God's word whole heartedly.

We should be quick to obey. The word of the Lord is precious. Though we may not understand it completely, we must hide it in our hearts. Rebekah knew God and knew the power of prayer. This mother-to-be carefully hid God's word deep in her heart.

Rebekah most certainly shared this information with Isaac but neither may have realized the magnitude of that word at the time. Isaac and Rebekah knew they were covenant people, fully aware they were promise holders but quite likely unable to anticipate the struggle that would ensue in this small family, probably oblivious to how it would impact future generations. Until now, they had been unaware she was carrying twins. They were simply happy she was pregnant! Now they learn there are TWO! Two sons! Two Nations?! Even better! What wonderful news!

ﮪﮪﮪ

The twin boys were born and the firstborn was named Esau. His name means *he that acts or finishes*. Jacob, the focal point of our story, was the second-born son. His name, meaning *heel grabber or supplanter* would testify to his personality as well as future events. They would later find this second born son overthrowing, tripping up and taking the place of his older brother in more than one way.

During childbirth, the younger Jacob reached out and grabbed hold of his brother, Esau's heel. The heel grabbing Jacob was guilty of at birth was notable enough to be recorded. It inspired his name and would be indicative of heel grabbing or supplanting in his adult life.

The two boys would display very different personalities. Jacob would mature to be a plain man. Unadorned and simple would describe him. He stayed close to home and close to mother; his personality closer to that of his father Isaac than his spirited mother Rebekah. Esau, was a cunning hunter; clever, shrewd and worldly. He was a great deal more like his adventurous mother than his laid back father, Isaac.

How early did these personality differences manifest? We do not know and we also are not completely sure whether the differences were obvious from the beginning. Were they possibly encouraged or in some way even orchestrated by a mother who was clinging to a word from God?

⌁⌁⌁

As the twins grew, Rebekah watched to see how the Lord would bring about His word. Was she guilty of manipulating to bring it to pass? It is possible she recognized characteristics and traits in the boys that helped her to identify the reasons why God had spoken as he did. It is also possible that the understanding of God's will for their lives remained a mystery until the boys embarked on manhood. We can only wonder in the early years whether or not she set about to influence the outcome. We can only speculate whether this word from the Lord proved to be a source of torment or comfort to Rebekah as her boys developed.

When you think about the words spoken over your own children, do you ever find yourself attempting to 'help' God? Meaning well, we can certainly get in the way more than help when it comes to the path God desires for our children. The wayward child may appear to be the one who needs a little guidance or a helping hand in fulfilling the word of God, when in fact, that waywardness is producing in them exactly what God intends. The child who is outwardly rebellious naturally receives more attention than the one who appears more compliant. While the compliant, obedient one may actually be the one in the most spiritual danger.

PLAYING FAVORITES

Struggling in the womb may have indicated trouble between Jacob and Esau but something perpetuated problems between the two. The Bible clearly says in Gen 25:27-28 that Isaac loved Esau but Rebekah loved Jacob. This was indicative of absolute favoritism.

Jacob and Esau were twins but complete opposites. They were dissimilar in temperament and occupation. Esau was worldly and enjoyed staying on the go. Travel was his favorite companion and recreation his most soothing rest. His business was to be about his business under the stars and away from home.

Isaac loved Rebekah. She was beautiful, boisterous and free spirited. That free spirit demonstrated on the first day she and Isaac met was apparently evident in Esau. Maybe it was the guts and gumption Esau possessed that caused Isaac to admire him so much.

The Bible says Isaac loved Esau because of the food he ate and prepared. He must have been some cook but he would have to learn a few things when he spent so much time so far from mama's kitchen. Maybe Esau reminded Isaac of his mother, Sarah, who had the wherewithal to force his father to put the bondwoman and her son out of their house, thereby enabling Isaac to have a far more peaceful existence.

Jacob was a shepherd by trade and we know that he would later bring his children up in the safety of this occupation. His preference was to stay close to home. He did not care about looking good or standing before people outside his intimate circle. Preferring his privacy, his safe-haven and likely the conversation of the animals under the blue sky, Jacob was likely a well-meaning man. His focus was probably more toward spiritual matters though we do not know whether this was partially due to his mother's upbringing or simply a demonstration of his personality. We are aware though, that early on, biblical mothers had a great deal of influence on their children.

Jacob almost certainly reminded Rebekah of Isaac, who was somewhat of a homebody, quiet and mild-mannered. Isaac, like Jacob, did not have a go-getter type of personality. This likely left room for her creative coercion in matters of importance.

Did preference and prejudice develop because Rebekah knew Jacob was God's chosen above his older brother Esau or was it due to some penchant for personality? Maybe Rebekah loved and chose whom the Lord loved since she was the one who had received the Word regarding the two boys as they struggled within her. Maybe she found Jacob's personality more attractive since he was so much like his father. Was it simply Rebekah's favoritism or had the word she heard from God built her faith and prevented her from compromising the integrity of it?

Sometimes the very things we love the most about our spouse can also become the things we like the least. It was possible Rebekah had grown to resent Isaac's lackadaisical attitude toward life. Rebekah may have been keenly aware of both the power of the promise and Isaac's contentment in going nowhere and doing nothing with it. What a waste!

Was Rebekah's favoritism toward Jacob a rejection of self? Maybe she saw herself and all her shortcomings in Esau and therefore favored Jacob? If she disliked and interpreted as less than ideal the rambunctious, rowdy, unsettled nature she possessed, Esau may have been a blatant reminder of those traits.

Who can say for sure why one was favored over the other by either parent. Who can say what their thoughts were regarding each other or how they felt inwardly about themselves. The real question; did either of them see the favoritism they bestowed upon the other child was wrong?

Ultimately, Rebekah's motive may have been right but her method slightly flawed. Or maybe her method and motive were right on cue according to God's plan. Maybe both left something to be desired. We cannot know for sure but we know the family. Isaac, Rebekah, Esau or Jacob, it does not matter. All of them were players in this biblical equivalent of a Broadway production. All were responsible.

The truth of the matter is this; God had a plan for the family and none of them, nor anyone or anything would ratify or nullify the covenant promise made long ago.

JACOB'S PASSIVE PERSONALITY-NO DRAMA MAMA'S BOY

As mentioned before, Jacob was not a man given to action. He was an uncomplicated man who enjoyed the effortless life of tending cattle. Cattle are not usually in a hurry to get anywhere, unless stampeded, and neither was Jacob. Evidently Jacob was the quiet type, who demonstrated a peaceful disposition and was satisfied to live a quiet and peaceable life at home. This apparently worked for him for the most part during his early life. Until he reached his seventies, his life had been largely void of drama. Favored by his mother, he was satisfied with the status quo. The trouble is; many times these are the ones you have to watch.

We must be cautious as passivity can cause us to miss our destiny in more than one way. When we are too passive, we can be easily bullied and manipulated. An attitude that we should not disappoint others causes us to be men pleasers rather than God pleasers. Often times, getting caught up in man-pleasing ultimately can produce an underlying anger within as we want to do what the Lord has called us to do but do not seem to possess the power within to overcome. Also, passivity may develop into more of a passive-aggressive nature and bring out behaviors that cause us to act out in fleshly behavior and even begin manipulating others to bring about a desired result. Passive-aggression can happen when we find ourselves unable to be assertive, doing what God says above what man wants. We can be especially vulnerable when dealing with someone in a position of natural or spiritual authority as this is usually someone you esteem highly and respect greatly.

REBEKAH-A DRIVING FORCE

It appears that Jacob's passivity contributed to his mother Rebekah being the driving force behind him for much of his early life. Why? Maybe it was because of her early conversation with God. After all, it was according to God's edict that Jacob was to take the lead in this family. It appeared Rebekah intended to do everything within her power to see that happen, even if Jacob was not one to take the initiative. Later we will see that Jacob was in fact the one who initiated the coup in the family and too that is was only after Rebekah was out of the picture that God could effectively deal with him face to face.

What is the driving force behind you when it comes to your promise? Do you sit back and hope something happens? Are you pushing others aside to take what you feel is rightfully yours? Is someone else doing the driving in your life? Any of these extremes are likely not the way we should manage matters of covenant and contract, especially with God.

Sometimes it takes removal of well-meaning people, even family members in order for God to complete His work in us as well!

OLDER WILL SERVE YOUNGER

We already know that customarily, the younger of the two would be subservient to the older in the family. Aware the struggle for the upper hand between these brothers began in the womb, we know this would not be the case with Jacob and Esau.

Jacob's getting the better of his brother Esau commenced before they took their first breath or suckled at their mother's breast. That would continue until Jacob obtained the blessing providence might have held for Esau. Jacob would gain quite a reputation of deception, manipulation and out-doing.

Though God would continue to show himself faithful and in control throughout the process of Jacob's life, Jacob would not make it easy. He managed again and again to resort to his own fleshly tactics not just to out-do his older brother but always looking for the easy way out. It was after many years and many bad decisions that he grew and finally matured.

Hostility would become the rule rather than the exception between brothers and between their descendants who would later be known as the Israelites and the Edomites. Why? Just as it was with Ishmael and Isaac, God had a plan and that plan involved mixing things up a bit.

This was not the only time God would go against the grain. In the line of the promised seed, God often chose the younger. This serves to override human tendency to believe that age or experience is the deciding factor in God's use of people to fulfill His purpose in the earth.

God chose Seth over Cain, Shem over Japheth, Isaac over Ishmael, Judah over Reuben, Manasseh over Ephraim. The only two in the line of promise whose brother's names are given who would be firstborn sons are Abraham and Jesus.

God's decision to turn the tables regarding Jacob and Esau perfectly highlights the fact that God's people are not subject to natural or worldly advancement but are products of sovereign, divine intervention. God has the right to do whatever He pleases and so He does.

So many remain perplexed at how a good God could allow certain things to happen or how such horrible tragedy could be of any use. All too often we use our strength to fight against the process rather than embracing what God has brought and simply obeying what he tells us.

It is not about your place in the family. It is not about whether you are good or bad. It is not about your social status, career, vehicle, clothes, family name, spouse, friends, success or lack thereof and it is most definitely NOT about works.

What is it about? It's about God bringing us to a place of willingness to accept and follow the process He has laid out for us in order that we carry out the covenant plan he has designed and thereby bring Him glory through it all!

Before Jacob and Esau were born, neither had done good or evil. They had not exhibited faith or rebellion. God's decision to elevate Jacob rather than Esau was not because of anything he had done to deserve it, nor was it because Esau had done anything to eliminate himself.

It was not due to works or faith or lack thereof but was *of Him that calleth* (Romans 9:11). It was that God's purpose in election might stand. It was because God had said so!

Now, we will see that Jacob's faith and works would eventually present themselves in both positive and negative ways. The process by which they would develop is what we must grab hold of if we are to understand, accept and use for good the difficult, sometimes horrific things we go through in our lives. It is a lesson we learn from his life as we move forward and claim our God given promise!

CHAPTER 2

Family Ties and Little White Lies

THE SALE OF THE BIRTHRIGHT

AS STATED EARLIER, Jacob's name means supplanter. His name means one who displaces and Jacob would come to be identified with deception. He had come from a family where 'white lies' were told when deemed necessary to save one's own skin. His grandfather Abraham had told lies regarding Sarah, his grandmother. Abraham said she was his sister. The justification? She was so beautiful he might be killed in order that they might obtain her. His father, Isaac had done exactly the same thing regarding his mother. Fearing death, he tried to pass Rebekah off as his sister. Both men's sin was exposed. To his chagrin, the deception and trickery that plagued Jacob's life would also be exposed.

The first indication of the character defects in Jacob surfaced when he used food and his brother's weakened condition to attain Esau's birthright. Did he manipulate his brother Esau into selling him his birthright? Was he somehow justified in doing so? After all, if Esau did not care enough to stay around family, home and his family business, then did he not deserve to lose it? Besides, Jacob did not steal it. He bought it, fair and square; for a bowl of beans from a hungry Esau all too eager to sell.

Jacob's desire of the birthright and his attainment of it did not match what Esau knew of his character. Though he may have had issues with the truth, he did not seem the type to be so bold as to go against Esau. He was usually quiet and compliant in nature. Since Jacob often hung out at home with his mother, Esau likely saw him as weaker than himself and assumed their deal would mean little in the whole scheme of things. Little did Esau know, though plain and simple, there was a thread that ran through Jacob's character that would stop at nothing to attain what God had in store for his life.

Jacob was the one most concerned with what was going on at home. Jacob was the one concerned with their future, looking out for aging parents and running the family business. It was likely not out of pride or ambition though, that he coveted the birthright. It was probably a spiritual eye for the promise and all the spiritual blessings that came with it. Rebekah may have planted these thoughts and ideas or hinted along the way that it would and should all be his one day, still, the manner in which he went about acquiring the birthright was craftier than he was known for being.

Though we refer to Jacob's acquisition of the birthright as stealing, the fact is, Jacob was direct and straightforward regarding this issue. Probably there had been some previous communication between the brothers concerning the matter. Jacob's desire for the birthright was likely not as big as surprise to Esau as it may seem when we read it. Esau may have on occasion spoken slightly regarding his birthright and all it entailed. When Jacob spoke of the matter on this occasion, pressing Esau to sell the birthright, Esau must have been thinking or maybe even verbalized, *You want all of THIS? Whatever! Not a problem! You can have it!* Esau's nonchalant attitude regarding such a serious issue likely encouraged Jacob to feel justified in his proposal. Esau held the birthright by providence but it was Jacob's according to promise. It is understandable how Jacob might not feel badly about acquiring something so vast for such a small price if it seemed the holder of it were unappreciative.

Esau was worldly. He had seen and experienced many things that Jacob had not. Jacob was without the same type of worldly wisdom but what Esau failed to realize is, people like that are sometimes the wisest of all. Their wisdom comes from another world in other ways. Rather than giving Esau a chance to get his belly full and rethink his decision, Jacob seized the opportunity when it presented itself and confirmed the transaction with an oath. *Swear to me this day!* Jacob made Esau swear that he would stand by that statement later. Esau had no problem doing so. At least he was in agreement at that time. Whether Esau was truly so hungry at the time that he could not go another minute without food or he simply thought Jacob would never hold him to his end of the bargain is not clear. Either way, from God's perspective, the transfer of power was comprehensive and all-inclusive.

This relatively easily acquired birthright packed a powerful punch for Jacob's future. It gave him superior rank in the family, according to Gen 49:3, a double portion of the paternal inheritance, according to Deut. 21:17, the priestly office in the family, according to Numbers 8:17-19, and the promise of the Seed by which all nations of the earth would be blessed according to Gen. 22:18.

Rebekah would fuel Jacob's later acquisition and it would seem she had to push him to get him to move but it appeared that Jacob set up and executed this earlier plan completely without aid. Though Rebekah probably would have liked to take the credit for this situation, she cannot. Jacob acted entirely on his own. The right to inheritance of everything the family owned and controlled, purchased for a bowl of beans? A sworn verbal agreement that could not be broken; what more could Jacob ask? How much easier could it be for the laid-back, slow-moving, smooth-talking Jacob?

What caused Esau to give up so much so easily? He was living in the moment. He was only concerned with today. His focus was on instant gratification. Esau was unknowingly in the perfect position to be taken advantage of. Though he did not realize it at the time, he traded short-term gain for long-term pain. He was weary from his journey. He was ravenously hungry and Jacob could see he was famished. He had undoubtedly been out in the wilderness for an extended period of time, as he often was and may have been unsuccessful in his hunting on this particular occasion.

Esau was a grown man. Coming from this covenant family he knew a verbal agreement was binding but this was his younger brother. There was no way Jacob would hold him to the agreement he made under such extreme circumstances. Jacob did, however, hold Esau to the verbal agreement for the birthright.

Do we allow weariness to make us a target for other's opportunism? We must be careful not to become weary (Gal. 6:6-9) and allow ourselves to be taken advantage of. We must be mindful of tomorrow. (Luke 12:19-20). There is very real cost for you and I, just as there was to Esau. Like Esau, we will be held to our hasty, thoughtless, misspoken words. We will pay the cost and suffer the consequences.

The cost for Esau's lost birthright? Everything! Jacob gained all the rights of the first-born though he was not. Had Rebekah shared her insight with her youngest son regarding his place in the family? We don't know but we do know this. Jacob, though quiet, was obviously scheming and planning how to get to the top! Jacob certainly had his mind on HIS future. Inside the quiet, mild-mannered Jacob, the wheels were turning and the focus was on SELF. Was this necessary? Not really. God would elevate Jacob regardless. Jacob was chosen. How would that have come forth? We do not know. We only know that it would have and it did.

Are there situations in your life that you know God has chosen you but you have forged ahead on your own and in your own strength? Like a rambunctious toddler crossing the street you refuse to take the hand of God and walk with Him into the promises prepared for you. Oh, the consequences of impetuous, impulsive and impatient behavior!

The Bible says Esau despised his birthright. We must be careful not to despise our birthright. 2Peter 3-4 says it is important that we do not despise where we come from. The people who beget us, the area we are brought up in, the quirks and idiosyncrasies of our families all work together as a part of a process that eventually brings us to fruition in the promised position.

It was not so much Esau's misdeed but his lack of remorse or repentance that sunk him. Esau was a man who placed his life in jeopardy every day by his career choice. He was a hunter in the desert and this was a very dangerous occupation. Stress was not new to Esau but Esau chose to make a permanent decision in a temporary stressful situation. He should have thought it through. *Will I feel different when my stomach is full? Is there something else to satisfy my hunger at this moment? Is it really worth it to give up so much for so little?* Instead, of evaluating the situation, Esau ate and drank to please his palate not giving a second thought to selling his birthright. He satisfied his appetite and then carelessly rose up without giving his condition a second thought. He did not seem at all to regret the bad bargain he had made. He despised his birthright and his actions of neglect, contempt and justification show a clear lack of remorse and absolutely no repentance of heart.

We are sometimes guilty of making permanent decisions during temporary stresses. Many times, those decisions cost us dearly. Sadly, we too rise up and walk away from a bad spiritual bargain as if there are no consequences. We are so relieved to be relieved of the symptoms of discomfort that we cannot see what we have really allowed. Stresses are usually temporary, a part of the process to give us understanding. Not a time to be making permanent decisions. We should rely on God as our radar to get us through and move only when we are divinely instructed. If we find we have done so, a repentant and contrite heart is the best path back to God's course of completion.

Had Esau been thinking long-term rather than allowing hunger pangs to consume his thoughts and actions, he might have given some thought to Jacob's proposition and decided the trade was not worth it. Esau's problem was not really his hunger but it was his total disregard for the physical and spiritual position God had placed him in. God knew this ahead of time and thus the choosing of Jacob. The priesthood of his family, their home, occupation and relationships were all quite unimportant to Esau. The only thing Esau was interested in was getting back out in the wild.

The Bible does not say why Esau had this attitude but if you take a moment and reflect on your memories of the last family get-together, or reunion you attended, you may understand a little better. If there are no embarrassing uncles, half-witted aunties, derelict dads or incarcerated cousins, then skip these next few lines. For the rest, read on.

The entire family was a little dysfunctional to say the least. Honesty and integrity were not their most outstanding personality traits. They had in laws, character flaws and everything else you can imagine. A rather eccentric grandfather, a spirited mother who favored his lying, *mama's boy* brother and no real place to call home were who Esau called family. No Thank you. He would rather be in the wild with the animals. There is more devotion and allegiance in the untamed wild than there was with these folks. Own, be the leader of, or more importantly be responsible for all of this? *No thanks!*

THE STOLEN BLESSING

Jacob moves ahead to insure the selling of the birthright of Esau is official. Now that Jacob had Esau's birthright, the need to acquire the family blessing becomes a priority. Time is getting short and we must remember each parent had their favorite and Isaac's was Esau.

Whether or not he knew about the sale of the birthright, we do not know but most likely the news had made its way to him. Did Esau tell him? Probably not; it was likely learned through Rebekah's wifely chatter regarding family issues, spiritual matters and God's plan for their sons. She probably added a complaint or two about Esau's total disregard for his family ties. It may have been Jacob who told Isaac in hopes of gaining favor and blessing outright from his aging father.

REBELLIOUS JACOB

Jacob was in his seventies and should have had a reputation of established character but his conduct was more like that of an immature and rebellious adolescent. A revolt of rebellion in his passive-aggressive heart and a little nudge from his life coach mother made for an imprudent combination. He had acquired the birthright openly. With reckless Rebekah promoting, provoking and pushing, he would soon procure the blessing of firstborn in a somewhat less than forthright manner.

Esau harbored a rebellion of his own which he demonstrated when he chose to marry more than one woman. This was proof he both disregarded the principle of monogamy and the principle to marry one who believed in the one true God. Both Isaac and Rebekah were very upset that Esau would make such an imprudent choice but tragically, Isaac does not make any real attempt to prevent Esau from marrying in this manner. The Bible says that *they*, probably Esau AND his wives quarreled with Isaac and Rebekah and rebelled against religious instruction. Yet, we soon see that Isaac remains resolved to give Esau the patriarchal blessing!

Oh, beware of rebellion. If yielded to, it will take hold and forever lock us into the place we first rebelled. It will manufacture such drama in our life that apprehension and nervousness will drive anxiety levels to the point of collapse. We will make foolhardy decisions, if we make decisions at all. They will alter our lives and prove counterproductive and destructive. We will walk out of one dilemma only to walk into another.

Rebellion convinces you that you are exempt from the rules and will ultimately force you away from everything and everyone you deem precious. Such would be the case for Jacob. One thing rebellion does not do? It does *not* negate the covenant. It cannot wipe out, destroy, annihilate or obliterate what God has promised.

ISAAC CALLS FOR ESAU

Isaac was getting old and he knew it. After all, he was sixty years old when the boys were born! If Isaac knew Jacob had the birthright, he does not tell but we will assume so because in all likelihood Rebekah long ago shared the word God had spoken to her about these two boys and their future. Isaac's favoritism toward Esau though, apparently inspired him to attempt a secretive impartation of blessing to Esau.

Usually, the time of blessing was done with family as witnesses, but Isaac called his eldest son to him without alerting anyone else. It appears Isaac planned to surreptitiously pass the blessing to Esau knowing full well that Jacob was the one God had chosen to lead the family after his death.

One must wonder if he really thought he was near the end or if he simply chose an opportune time to get by with this scheme because the Bible records that Isaac lives decades beyond this point.

While still somewhat cognizant or maybe not so much so, Isaac decided to manipulate the situation. The difficult thing to understand is why Isaac would want to give Esau the blessing after the way he and his heathen wives were behaving? The blessing was for the promised Seed. This, Isaac knew full well. Did he think blessing Esau would change his rebellious behavior thereby changing the course of things? Or knowing that Jacob was the one with whom the covenant stood, did he think the only way Esau would receive any inheritance at all was through this type of underhanded passing of the blessing?

REBEKAH OVERHEARS ISAAC

Isaac's underhanded intentions would not go unnoticed by the woman of the house though. Listening around corners and manipulation of events seemed to be a part of normal routine for this family originating from way back and it just so happened that Rebekah overheard Isaac and Esau's conversation.

Do you think Rebekah suspected Isaac's plan previously and paid close attention to any interaction with his son? Was the favoritism so obvious toward Esau that she knew Isaac would never give the blessing to Jacob as God intended? Well. No matter. She had a plan to make things right, in spite of her husband's lack of forthrightness but she must act quickly. Isaac had sent Esau out to the field and he would not be gone long.

Rebekah, along with Jacob, decided to seize the opportunity to obtain the blessing by taking advantage of Isaac's age and failing senses. Rebekah knew Jacob was the one God had chosen to carry the promise and so did Isaac. Whether it was the bad memory of old age or the will to do as he pleased that incited Isaac to attempt to pass the blessing to the one he favored, it was not a problem for Rebekah. She would simply take matters into her own hands and proceed to right the situation. Together, Jacob and his mother would seize the opportunity to take full advantage of his brother's absence and his father's infirmity.

As Jacob had little ambition on his own, the real catalyst for his acquiring the blessing was Rebekah. She was careful to insist that he obey her without hesitation and do exactly as she instructed him. This was tricky business. Not only did the plan have to be carried out in a hurry, there was no way to know whether or not they would be successful. *What if Esau came back early? What if Isaac recognized Jacob?* The uncovering of their plot would ruin everything. Both Rebekah and Jacob would be exposed for the deceitful, conniving pair that they were. Jacob seemed somewhat worried about the possibility of exposure.

What if he wants to touch me? Esau is hairy but I am not. What will happen if he touches me? I shall seem to him as a deceiver and will bring a curse upon myself rather than a blessing. I don't want to seem a deceiver. Never mind that I AM a deceiver and this IS deception. I just don't want to SEEM like one to my father. Otherwise, I will not be able to trick him into giving me the blessing. I do NOT want to be exposed.

REBEKAH-UPON ME BE THE CURSE-DO WHAT I SAY

Jacob did not disagree with his mother's plan and he did not mind to lie. He had certainly had experience in that area. He just did not want to *look* like a liar. He was simply afraid of getting caught. He was afraid of being exposed. He feared the repercussions if he was caught, not the spiritual ramifications even if he got away with it. It was apparent he did not mind the bittersweet taste of deception, only the stinging sensation of responsibility.

With time getting away from them, Rebekah promised to take the curse upon her, if he would simply hurry up and do what he was told. This seemed to satisfy Jacob. Relieved of all the responsibility of what was about to take place, Jacob obeyed his mother. Jacob acquired the meat. This solidified his willingness to participate in the devious plan. Rebekah acquired Esau's clothing and made a costume to insure Isaac would believe Jacob was Esau.

FAMILY TIES AND LITTLE WHITE LIES ❧

Now it was time for the meal! Rebekah made the food that Jacob would take to his father. She had either watched or maybe even taught Esau to cook for himself in the wild and it was what Isaac loved about Esau. She knew exactly what to do.

JACOB WENT IN-ISAAC QUESTIONS WHICH SON

As Jacob approached his father, dressed like his older brother, ailing Isaac question Jacob's identity. Jacob tells him, *I am Esau thy firstborn; I have done what you asked me to do. I beg you, sit and eat so that you can bless me.*

Isaac questions how he found game so quickly and Jacob tells him that Isaac's God (something Esau would say) brought it to him. The comment was misleading at best, but actually was downright deceptive. On some level, Isaac knew something was amiss. *Let me touch you to see if you are Esau or not.*

Isaac was uncertain and aware of Jacob's acquisition of the birthright, he may have expected to some extent that Jacob would try to mislead him. It was after all Jacob's nature. Not only that. It was a habitual practice in this family as Isaac himself was trying to deceive Jacob. In a family accustomed to deceit and drama, the trust level among them was extremely low.

The voice is Jacob's, Isaac says *but the hands are of Esau.* Couldn't he have touched his face to further investigate? Isaac continues to question whether he is speaking to the son he requested but he Bible says he discerned him not, because his hands were hairy. One more time he asks, *Art thou my very son Esau?* Jacob said *I am.* Jacob brought his father food and wine and he imbibed.

Isaac's favorite son was Esau and his intent was to bless Esau with the covenant blessing God had said belonged to Jacob. How is it he could not discern the difference between the two? Was he so old and so sick that he really could not tell the difference? Or was he ignoring all sense that he was being deceived because deep within, he knew what destiny held in this situation.

Now Isaac has eaten and drank a bit of wine. His belly is full and now he wants his son to come near him and kiss him. *See?* He says. It seems as though Isaac is still attempting to convince himself that this is, in fact, Esau. *See?* The smell of my son is as the smell of a field which the Lord has blessed. Therefore, God give the dew of heaven, the fatness of the earth and plenty of corn and wine.

LET THY MOTHER'S SONS

Gen 27:28 NIV says *therefore, may God give you of the dew of heaven, of the fatness of the earth, and plenty of grain and wine. Let peoples serve you, and nations bow down to you. Be master over your brethren, and let your mother's sons, bow down to you. Cursed be everyone who curses you, and blessed be those who bless you!*

Part of the blessing was that the people would serve him, the nations would bow to him and he would be lord over his brethren. We must not overlook the next part though; and let thy mother's sons bow down to thee. Who might he be referring to? Well, Jacob, of course. Or so he thinks.

Sounds a bit like a curt way of saying, your mother's favorite son will be forced to bow to you. *Her son. You know, the one always hanging on her skirt tail. Remember him? This is the son who can do no wrong as far as she is concerned. He is the soft son, the plain son, the quiet son. Jacob. Let JACOB bow down to thee.* And cursed be everyone that curseth thee and blessed be the ones who bless thee.

Hearing these words spoken by his own father must have been

hurtful to Jacob and likely made him all the more determined to complete his deceptive task.

➤➤➤

Barely out of Isaac's tent was Jacob before Esau came home. No doubt Esau was anxious to do as his father told him, if for no other reason than to surpass his brother. Jacob may have bought his birthright, and Esau may be legally bound to relinquish this birthright but the blessing would pack a powerful punch and it was about to be his! Esau was completely unaware he had been hoodwinked by his mother and his younger brother.

The silence must have been deafening in between Esau's petition for Isaac to arise and eat and Isaac's response. *WHO are you? ESAU? Where is the one who brought venison earlier? Remember? I ate it and I blessed him. Oh, and yes, he shall be blessed. It was the blessing of all blessings. It is irrevocable, complete, unyielding. The blessing I bestowed upon him is the blessing I had in store for my favorite son. It is the blessing I had for you Esau This blessing came from the heart of my being and now it belongs to Jacob!*

Esau cried a bitter cry and for the first time, it appeared he was vulnerable as he begged his father to bless him also. Isaac knew the magnitude of what had transpired and all he could do was explain that Jacob had gotten both of their blessings. Isaac's intent was to bestow this extra helping of blessing on his rebellious firstborn Esau but he had inadvertently given it to Jacob, leaving virtually NOTHING for Esau!

ONE BLESSING FOR ME?

Esau immediately realizes the significance of what has happened. *Is he not rightly named Jacob? He has displaced me these TWO times! He took away my birthright and now my blessing!*

Esau pleads with Isaac. *Father, please tell me you have reserved a blessing for me. Please tell me that he has not acquired all that should have been mine in the first place. I am older now and I realize what I did when I nonchalantly gave up my birthright but please, please tell me I have not lost my blessing as well.*

Isaac proceeds to tell his eldest son that he has not only made him his Lord, he has also given Jacob all his brethren as servants and sustained him with wine and corn. *What is left to give you, my son?* Esau continues weeping and begging for just ONE blessing!

Gen 27:39-40 And Isaac his father answered and said unto him, Behold, thy dwelling shall be the fatness of the earth, and of the dew of heaven from above. And by thy sword shalt thou live, and shalt serve thy brother, and it shall come to pass when thou shalt have dominion, that thou shalt break his yoke from off thy neck.

Esau was desperate. He could not let it go without his father giving him some type of blessing. *Something, anything, please!* Isaac tells Esau, your dwelling shall be the fatness of the earth and the dew from heaven, you will live by your sword and shall serve your brother and it shall come to pass when you have dominion, power, control, dominance, that you will break his yoke, burden, repression, bondage from off thy neck. Esau wasn't very receptive to a blessing that simply seemed to restate the obvious. HE would serve his younger brother and continue to be forced to make his living from the land as he had chosen to do in his youth. Not only that but when he had the upper hand, he was to release his brother and himself from bondage!

ESAU PLOTS AGAINS JACOB

There was *no* comfort for Esau in this blessing and he hated Jacob because of what he had lost. Esau's determination was exactly as his father had said. One day I will be in control, have dominion, power, dominance and then Jacob will see. *Only, I will kill him! I will wait until the days of my father are finished and then I will kill him! This will automatically put the family and all we own back into my hands.*

Esau failed to realize that the burden placed on his neck from the situation with Jacob would be a requirement to forgive and move on. Later, when it would seem that Esau could finally get the better of Jacob, God would not allow it.

CHAPTER 3

Running For Your Life

REBEKAH DISCOVERS ESAU'S PLAN TO KILL JACOB

ESAU'S THREAT TO slay his brother made its way to their mother. Apparently, no one knew she had anything to do with the stolen blessing and you can be assured, she was not confessing. What she did do? She quickly called for Jacob to forewarn him of Esau's plan.

Who really knew how long Isaac had to live. He was old and ailing but Esau determined, the minute my father is gone, *I will kill Jacob.* This was information Jacob needed.

Rebekah must now come up with yet another plan but first, she must alert Jacob. She calls him in to tell him that his brother has found a way to comfort himself. *Jacob, Esau is going to KILL you! Now, son, once again I need you to obey without question. Go to your uncle Laban's house in Haran and stay there a few days until your brother calms down a little. Soon Esau will go back to the field, back to what he loves most and he will forget what you have done to him.* Jacob must have thought – *What I have done to him?! This is what YOU told me to do mother!*

Rebekah's maneuver to get Jacob to leave was classic motherly manipulation. If he would not leave to save his own skin, maybe he would leave to make mama feel better. Rebekah plays on Jacob. *Why should I be deprived of both of you in one day? How can I lose your father and you at the same time? I simply could not bear this to happen.*

Though it likely did not take much encouragement, Rebekah convinces Jacob to listen to her once again and take a four hundred mile trip on foot to Laban, her brother's house and choose a wife from among his cousins. Oh, great! Is that not always what controlling mothers think is the answer for their pathetic, pathological liar sons? Run away from your problems and find a woman to fix you and make you feel better when the truth and its trouble finally catch up to you.

Jacob, unlike his brother Esau, had a non-confrontational nature, remember? Being ever the one to avoid conflict, it did not take much for Jacob to agree with Rebekah's strategy. This sort of person is always ready and willing to find someone to tell them what to do. This insures they will not be held responsible when their world comes crashing down around them.

With Rebekah's plan, Jacob will not have to trouble himself with when or how to return home, as Rebekah will alert him when it is alright to come back. All Jacob need do, is concern himself with finding a wife. He will go to family. Therefore he will not have to worry about starting over with nothing and in the process will find a wife. Rebekah, as usual, will manage everything else. This gives Jacob time to ponder not the condition of his character, or the consequences of his actions but the most significant thing in his life, *his desires!*

Though it may have looked as if Rebekah was willing to take the heat, the truth is, neither Jacob nor Rebekah intended to take responsibility for their actions. Accountability was not an option!

Esau is hot under the collar but Rebekah seems to think a little time and distance between brothers will remedy this upheaval and help him to get over it. Then, life will continue as usual. Jacob's little vacation will give Esau time to cool off. Maybe Esau will head back out to the countryside. Rebekah will then send for Jacob. When she sees that Esau's fury has subsided and he has not only forgiven but forgotten the magnitude of what Jacob did to him, she will let Jacob know it is okay to return. *Give it a little time and this storm will blow over.* Or so she thinks. At the time Rebekah did not realize the extent of Esau's fury. But for now, it's time to convince Isaac her plan is a good idea.

REBEKAH'S PLAN TO SAVE JACOB

We already know Rebekah had no more intention than Jacob of taking responsibility for her actions. First, she went to Jacob and told him what to do. Then she went to Isaac and manipulated him into making the same choice as if it were *his* idea. You can imagine how it must have sounded. *Isaac, these women are not good enough for my Jacob. If Jacob takes one of the women from this land, what good is my life? I've tried so hard to bring him up right and this would destroy all that hard work.* She probably added the sidebar of the blessing he now carried to support her case. Jacob would likely now be considering a wife and family. With all of that responsibility, the wife he chose was now more important than ever. The only thing that made sense was for Jacob to go to Laban's.

It likely made sense to Isaac as well. It was apparent Esau did not want to trouble his aging father with his murderous plans toward his brother, so Isaac probably believed it was exactly as Rebekah presented it. Though Isaac probably sensed tension in the air, not being one who enjoyed confrontation, he probably never mentioned it.

ISAAC'S CHARGE TO JACOB REGARDING ABRAHAMIC COVENANT

If Jacob went away, it would be better for the entire family. Who knows how Isaac felt toward Jacob right now. Was he angry? Hurt? Disappointed? Resigned? Relieved? Perhaps Isaac thought, *soon I'll be gone and then what will happen?* Rebekah could not be left with the drama that was likely to occur between the two boys if Jacob stayed. What was done was done. It was decided that Jacob would leave for his uncle's house and Isaac now blessed Jacob, as Jacob.

Do not take a wife of the daughters of Canaan. Go to your uncle Laban's house. Be fruitful and multiply. God gave that land to Abraham and to thee, and to thy seed with thee.

Isaac did not mention himself in this blessing. He mentioned Abraham and then Jacob. Abraham had been given the original covenant promise. Isaac carried it but as with Abraham, it would not be fulfilled through him alone. Jacob signified the future of the covenant. Isaac may have had regrets over time lost or imprudent decisions as many do at the end of their time here on earth, but there was still hope for Jacob.

Though it was Isaac's desire to pass the blessing to Esau, it was through Jacob the promise would be carried out. And so, Isaac sent Jacob away with yet another blessing. Good thinking. He had heard the anguish in Esau's voice regarding the blessing given to Jacob. Isaac knew there would be trouble and he was not in a position to do much about it. He must do what *his* passive nature would always default to; try to keep the peace. *Yes, leaving is a good idea. Go Jacob. Go with my blessing. Go with God's blessing.*

JACOB ESCAPES ESAU

This journey would take Jacob into an unknown country, into unfamiliar territory, where he would be living with people, though related, who are strangers to him. The deceitfully acquired blessing creates uneasiness and a displacement from his comfort zone rather than confidence of pleasure and prosperity for the future. It is not long before he realizes, he has stepped over a line.

Jacob, driven by the desires of his beloved mother and his own lack of integrity and initiative, finds himself on an unfamiliar road traveling at an out of control speed. His unpretentious life now seems extremely complicated.

Imagine allowing deception to dominate your decisions until your very existence is reduced to misery. A lifestyle such as this produces a mind-set of continuously conspiring and scheming to attain something for nothing.

As Jacob evaluates his new assignment it is quite disturbing. He now has to face his future without the wisdom and guidance of his father, the unconditional support of his mother and without the companionship of his brother. If only he had thought the whole thing through.

Little did Jacob know; a few days would turn into decades before he returned home. He did not know it at that time but he would bury his father and would never see his mother again. What a price the entire family would pay for their sin.

Although Jacob's ill-obtained acquisition of the blessing had revealed a conniving, deceitful character and a lack of motivation, he had one thing going for him; Jacob was covenant seed. Isaac's son, Abraham's grandson! He was the product of a blood covenant between God and his grandfather. This covenant was reaffirmed with his father and was irrevocable regardless of Jacob's lifestyle. He was marked by blood and this changed everything. There were blood covenant promises hovering over his life. This promise was a pledge by a holy God who does not change. Reversal was out of the question.

WHEN ESAU SAW WHAT DISPLEASED ISAAC – HE DID IT

When Esau saw that Isaac had further blessed Jacob and sent him away to find a wife and Jacob obeyed, Esau was even more furious! Talk about adding insult to injury! The anger and resentment Esau must have felt toward Isaac at that moment were enough to push him over the edge! When he saw that the daughters of Canaan were exactly what Isaac did *not* want for his sons, he went straight to Ishmael and found himself more wives.

Remember Ishmael, Isaac's half-brother? Ishmael was sent away so that he would not share in the inheritance with Isaac but that did not matter to Esau. This was *the* thing his father did not want his sons to do. Therefore, it was *the* thing Esau *determined* to do. This was not the first time Esau hung out with the wrong crowd against his parent's wishes. This root of rebellion was exactly why Esau did not need to be the one to carry the covenant. Though Jacob appeared to be the deceptive one and the wayward deceiver, Esau harbored a rebellion that rivaled all others. He would ultimately find himself on the outside of the covenant as had Ishmael.

EMOTIONS OF PARENTS REGARDING JACOB LEAVING

I am sure that when Isaac and Rebekah sent Jacob off to Laban's there were many emotions to deal with. Their deceptive son was now on his way out of their lives, at least for a while. Was it a good day for Isaac? Was he relieved to get who he perceived to be the problem out of the house?

After all, it is extremely difficult dealing with a rebellious child. The lying, the manipulating the constant drama of it all is draining and sometimes just to get them out of the house is enough for at least a small reprieve. Trouble is, these feelings of relief when the trouble is gone from the house can be quite bittersweet. The peace is welcomed but the break in relationship and the circumstances that caused the situation in the first place leave behind a residue of heartache that is difficult to manage.

After all, it was not supposed to be like this, now was it? We are supposed to be pleased for our children when they grow and mature and we send them off with blessing, knowing they will return another day to share in the love and joy of family celebration and reunion. We are not prepared for the flood of emotion when finally the irresponsible, unruly, immature child is out of the house and the door is slammed behind them.

Isaac and Rebekah or parents today, time and setting completely different, yes but parental matters of the heart are similar. The desire for our children to prosper is the same. The hope for family to live harmoniously is not so different at all.

Oh, the condition of this family! Rebekah must have laid in bed at night and agonized. This family, this mother, father and children were experiencing so much loss so quickly. How did this get so out of control? The strain on the relationship she shared with her beloved Isaac was upsetting at best. Rebekah not only lost her favorite son, she lost her relationship with her eldest son. Sometimes it is the meddling mother that has the most difficult time letting go; even when it is according to a plan she orchestrates.

HOW DID REBEKAH FEEL?

Early on, Rebekah had had a visitation from the Lord regarding these sons of hers. You have to wonder how many times, if ever she questioned that word. What an emotional vacillation between knowing the Lord had spoken to her concerning her children and wondering if she misunderstood or misinterpreted what He said. Was the pain of it unbearable for her causing her to scream a scream in her heart no one else could hear? Could God hear her scream from this place? Would this family ever be whole again?

As a mother, she undoubtedly mourned the loss of the love and rela-tionship between her two sons. Or maybe she wondered if there re-ally had ever been an authentic love between the two. It had always been a struggle between those two from the very moment of concep-tion. Reasoning for herself, she may have determined she could main-tain relationship with both sons and simply make sure they stayed separated. Then again, Jacob was going so far away. How could that work?

Rebekah perhaps strongly considered running after Jacob to stop him from leaving. Hoping to make one last attempt to resolve the issues with his brother, did she think there might be one more thing she could do or say? Maybe an appeal to Esau would reach his heart and stop this madness.

The anger and resentment hanging over the family due to Esau's rage toward his brother now threatened to force everyone to walk on egg-shells as long as Jacob remained in the house. Esau, knowing his mother favored Jacob may have been suspicious she was at the root of the deception, even though appeared spear-headed by Jacob. After all, everyone knew Jacob was not known for his plans of action.

Desperately trying to hold this thing together must have aged Re-bekah. It must have seemed as though she could look in the mirror and see herself getting older right before her very eyes. Life is so out of control. Here they were; no one with a heart of reason and no one with an eye for the future. Like many mothers, she must have asked herself how even God could work this one out.

Oh, the agony of regret. The worst thing was the torment of wonder-ing where she went wrong or *if* she went wrong? She was only hold-ing on to what the Lord had said. *Or was she?* Was she simply making an attempt to micromanage things in the way she saw fit? There was so much deception in the family maybe she had deceived herself the whole time! Surely she felt some culpability.

On the other hand, Rebekah may have inwardly justified her actions. Feeling as though she had obeyed God and everyone else simply could not see or understand her dedication.

We do not know if Rebekah realized that Jacob not only disregarded and disrespected his father and brother but also her. Jacob obviously loved himself above all. Rebekah may have convinced herself that he made his choices out of love for and obedience to her but the truth of the matter was; Jacob's choices were generally to placate others and/or to benefit Jacob.

How can a family with such strong promises from God fall to this low estate? How does this happen to a covenant family? Was it preventable? All the pain, the questioning and the fear that must have threatened to overtake them.

Oh, the suffering thoughts of the future fostered! Gone were the days of hope for happiness and unity within her family. It must have been difficult to put on a happy face in public, pretending that her husband was not old, dying and disillusioned with her. Ignoring whispers that her boys were at odds to the point of death. How difficult to hide the pain.

How do you find your way through the fog to that place? How do you get over these devastating losses in life? *How?* Is it that you grieve over the loss of what you had or do you ponder whether or not you ever had anything to lose in the first place? Do you grieve over what will never be? Have you been through such devastation that you simply grieve with no clear direction for your grief? The grief itself is horrendous, staggering and appalling!

Rebekah likely suffered alone. Undoubtedly, she had no one to talk to about her family's dilemma and drama. Surely she longed for someone. She was a woman who loved her husband and her children. Though she was a bit impetuous, she had nothing other than their best interest at heart.

After all, she was Abraham's daughter-in-law. They were people of promise and she longed to see that promise fulfilled. Here she was though; the father of faith as a father-in-law and her family falling apart. Trouble letting go of your child is not something you can talk to your family about when your husband's father was perfectly willing to lay him on an altar and sacrifice him at the command of God!

Abraham believed God would provide. Rebekah must have wanted to believe that as well. Abraham had faith enough to kill his son if the Lord required. He also had faith the Lord would raise him from the dead. He had already received him raised from the dead. So was the faith of Abraham.

It must have felt to Rebekah as though Jacob were dead. She must have realized that she could die, Isaac could die or his brother could choose to hunt him down and kill him anyway before he had opportunity to return.

No. Abraham would not be the one to talk to and neither would anyone who knows you are part of this family. Imagine the juicy gossip this would raise at church on Sunday? What would the neighbors think? Was this Rebekah's battle? Could she trust anyone? When you are the father of faith's daughter-in-law, who do you talk to about fear?

Rebekah's actions seemed less than forthright but necessary. If she had waited, Esau would have been the one blessed by Isaac and where would that have left Jacob, the promise holder? We know it is difficult for her to comprehend with her limited perspective and broken heart. It is easier to see God's plan at work from our vantage point. How fortunate that makes us. We have a bird's eye view into this family's struggle to walk in the promise of God. If we couple that with a willingness to listen and learn, we may avoid some of the heartbreaking pitfalls in our own walk.

Have you found yourself in similar situations? Can you understand some of the emotions experienced by this dysfunctional covenant family? If you have ever heard God and questioned the word He spoke when your life started to fall apart; yes, you can. The timing, the setting, the names; all different but the heartache and heart cries identical!

How often have you wondered how you can know without question you are blessed? Especially when you feel and maybe even look to others as if you are cursed? The blessing after all is a blessing on all of your seed! They are blessed and everyone after them is blessed; so many they cannot be numbered! How can this be a good thing when it seems this one seed is killing you!

How many times have you asked yourself *will the promise ever be fulfilled? Was there ever really a promise anyway? If this is really God and He is in control, then why am I hurting so badly? Why is my life devastated? How will I ever regain perspective and get back on my feet? Is following God always this hard? Where does all the suffering come in if I am a covenant child walking in the promise of God?* The struggle within is torment; the anxiety overwhelming. Constant questioning and anguish seem to be a way of life. Torment seems all there is or ever will be; torment and *fear!*

We don't really know what issues Rebekah struggled with. Whether she was afraid for herself or her family, whether she had regret for the day Isaac entreated the Lord for these two sons, whether she even once doubted God had told her the truth about the destiny of Jacob. We don't know if she ever once questioned, *God, if this is you, why is my family torn and why am I in such agony?* We only know what is recorded in the word. We only know her actions at the time and her family's response to them. We only know the favored son of Rebekah was gone and most likely, gone from her sight forever.

HOW DID ISAAC FEEL?

Jacob's quiet rebellion held this covenant family hostage with his underlying manipulation and control. His rebellion seemed unobtrusive but was potentially spiritually deadly. When Esau's rebellion was exposed it was according to his personality, more forthright and open. There seemed to be more self-restraint in Jacob but this is not really the case. It only appeared so.

Personality has so much to do with the manifestation of rebellion. It did with Jacob and Esau and it does with us as well. Placed in the right set of circumstances even a slow-talking laid back good ole boy will manifest rage. It may be a silent rage but it is rage nonetheless.

Nothing short of divine intervention will affect the spirit of rebellion. It is cruel, even ruthless. It will steal from parents or siblings as it had in this family. This is the least of what the spirit of rebellion will do to a family. The one operating in the spirit of rebellion will rule and ravage. The person who is rebellious will control the whole family and force all other acquaintances to accomplish all of their wants. No one else matters and they will stop at nothing. Rebellion manipulates and attempts to control everyone and everything in its path. The most out of control people are those with a controlling spirit. The Bible calls rebellion as the sin of witchcraft.

〰〰

Did Isaac sorrow and mourn over the condition of his son or his family? Did he ponder or agonize how his covenant family could have settled in this state or condition? How had things escalated to this place of wreckage? Isaac may have questioned God and undoubtedly questioned himself. Did he wrestle with feelings of failure or inquire of God what he might have done differently? In his mind, Rebekah may have shouldered the blame altogether, though he would likely never say so.

Isaac's inward security or lack of regarding Jacob's leadership of their family did not matter at the moment. He *was* the one God chose and Isaac knew it. What he likely felt at the moment was a sense of relief. Now he would not have to watch everything in the house in order for Jacob not to steal him blind or stand guard over Esau to keep him from killing his brother in anger.

Isaac may have inwardly sensed the inevitable train wreck down the track if change did not occur in Jacob. Was he ever in a place of struggle over a solution or did he know from the beginning it would take a visitation from God? Did Isaac have an accurate view of his sons and how they had progressed deeply into this way of life or was Isaac so old and his senses so dull that it escaped him? Was his eyesight the only thing dull or was his spirit dull by now? Maybe, Isaac was keenly aware of the spiritual condition of his entire family but unable to do anything about it. He may have been conniving and lazy as he might have appeared or maybe he simply trusted God.

No matter how Isaac felt about Jacob's leaving, Jacob *was* leaving. He was on his way to a far country. He had no idea of the plan of God when he first left but Isaac was possibly somewhat spiritually aware. Isaac was letting him go and he did not chase him down to make sure he got to where he was going. Like the father of the prodigal son, Isaac stayed home and allowed God to do the work in Jacob's heart. There was really no other way.

PART 2:

FROM UGLY LIFE TO UGLY WIFE

CHAPTER 4

Jacob's New Life And New Wife

JACOB STOPS FOR THE NIGHT-ROCK PILLOW

JACOB SET OUT and Gen 28:11 tells us he stopped for the night....
and he lighted upon a certain place, and tarried there all night, because the sun was set; and he took of the stones of that place, and put
them for his pillows and lay down in that place to sleep.

We look away now from all the gut-wrenching drama at home to
Jacob's first night away from home. He was running from an enraged
brother who vowed to kill him, a mother who got him into this mess
and a father that would likely die before he would lay eyes on him
again.

With stones for a pillow, the earth for his bed, the evening dew for a
comforter and the night sky for a canopy, Jacob probably quite be-
wildered, began to absorb the reality of his present condition. He
may have been so emotionally exhausted he went right off to sleep or
maybe he laid on the cool, damp earth with his head aching from the
hard rock supporting it, his heart pounding in his chest from anxiety,
pondering how he had managed to get himself into this mess.

He had to wonder; how does a descendant of Abraham, Isaac's son for heaven's sake, wind up in this fix? All of the sweet words of blessing he had received from his father when Isaac thought him to be Esau seemed of little or no value out here in the wilderness with only the stars for a ceiling. At home he would have been lying on quality bedding with soft pillows for his head. Alone and lonely, I imagine he questioned if that ill-obtained blessing was really worth this. He had never been this depleted before.

THE DREAM STAIRWAY

Emotionally drained and miserable, he falls asleep and dreams. Not a common dream but one divinely influenced by God. Through this dream, the Lord makes Jacob a promise and reveals Himself and a host of angels to him. Jacob was not expecting this. He knew God had visited his grandfather, Abraham and his father, Isaac but this is a different situation entirely.

However, God did not see it so differently at all. On Jacob's first night away from home he has a firsthand encounter with God. God promises not only that He will be with Jacob but will bring him again to his homeland. God speaks of Jacob's future giving him a vision to hold fast to. What refreshing news to a homebody like Jacob! His regrettable choices of late excluded him from the fellowship of family and friends. He probably felt excluded and forgotten as well as forsaken by all but God reassured him He would not leave him. No one had to explain to Jacob the meaning of this visitation.

Jacob wastes no time entreating God to guard, guide and provide. In awe, he declares, God is in this place and I knew it not. If he had been anticipating a meeting with God, he certainly would not have expected it would be at this place, or with his current condition. Jacob knew Isaac had sent him off to Padan-aram with the blessing of Abraham but as self-centered as Jacob was, he was so busy focusing on himself, he never imagined God would meet him in the middle of nowhere and have such a conversation.

Jacob was uncomfortable, feeling exposed and uneasy in this unfamiliar territory. Remember? Jacob was a mama's boy who never strayed far from home. Yet in this uncomfortable and unsettled place he had a very comforting dream; the covenant confirmed and the assurance God was and would remain with him.

To quote Matthew Henry *"God's time to visit His people with His comforts is when they are most destitute of other comforts and other comforters. When afflictions... do abound, then shall consolations so much more abound."*

Genesis 28:12 and he dreamed and behold a ladder set up on the earth, and the top of it reached to heaven and behold the angels of God ascending and descending on it.

A ladder; a huge ladder reaching from earth to heaven! The story of Jacob's ladder is well-known for many reasons. Many things are revealed each time it is shared, yet we will touch on only a few. The ladder in Jacob's dream was set up on the earth to assure Jacob that what is happening in the earth is fully known and orchestrated in heaven then carried out on earth under the guardianship of God almighty. This ladder revealed God's process, His ladder, His step by step plan that would prove to take Jacob straight into the fulfillment of the blessing he had received. Just when Jacob couldn't see where his future was headed, God made it plain to Jacob that no matter what had happened he really could acquire the promise from here!

We know that what is known in heaven AND earth does not escape the attention of God and His mighty hand of Judgment. This ladder is a representation of our process as well. Destiny is a process and must be followed and carried out step by step, or in this case wrung by wrung. God's wisdom is atop the ladder and the angels, who are God's ministering spirits, are continually ascending and descending, giving report to God. We should follow this example carefully. Why we do not go to God, receive blessing and instruction and promptly govern ourselves accordingly is a mystery. It would streamline life on earth significantly.

There is only one way to gain victory concerning life issues and that is God's way. His way involves a process that is to be carried out one step at a time. Jacob would navigate through many phases throughout his life. He would find himself uprooted more than once but always returning to a clearer path guided by God. This place, in the dark, in the middle of nowhere was only the beginning for Jacob.

WHAT GOD SAID TO JACOB

What God said to Jacob as he stood above this great ladder? *Jacob, I'm the God of your father Abraham and of Isaac. The land you're lying on? I'm giving it to you. Not just to you but your seed too. Oh, and by the way, there will be a bunch of them, spreading west, east, north and south. In you and yours Jacob, everyone on earth will be blessed. Not only that but I will keep you wherever you go and I'll bring you back to this land. Jacob, I won't leave you until I've done everything I've said.*

What God did NOT say to Jacob? *Look, Jacob. All I've said is true but this thing is going to take some time, not to mention a great deal of effort and change on your part. Most of it, you're not going to like and what you think it's supposed to look like, it won't. You're going to have to trust me. Take it as it comes. Embrace the difficult parts because they are the vehicle I plan to use to take you into this power and increase that I have promised. Oh yeah, and Jacob? Pick the ugly girl . . .*

Don't you just love the way God chooses to reveal the beautiful big picture? Revealing His promise in a wonderful, spiritual moment but the particulars of the process he will use to get us there come to light little by little, often times painstakingly! So maybe it is a bit easier to love it when it is happening to Jacob rather than in our own lives.

A visitation from God is altogether new to Jacob. He is very much aware of the class of human he really is and the issues he is dealing with. This visitation was entirely unexpected but welcomed by a man who had just lost everything and everyone near and dear. The idea of the God of the blessing showing up to encourage him personally was exactly what he needed.

God alone sets the appointment to manifest Himself to His wayward children. An encounter such as this changes a person, hence the beginning of real changes in Jacob. Not only did God reiterate the covenant and make a promise to Jacob, Jacob made a promise to God. He then worshipped Him with a solemn vow to give God the tithe. One tenth of all God blessed him with, he would return to Him.

Have you ever noticed when true change begins in the heart of a person they become willing to give God His money? There is a link to the heart and the wallet. Maybe this is because our money represents our life and when God has our heart, he has our life.

It is evident God is showing Jacob His goodness and it is the goodness of God that brings men to repentance. True repentance causes a man to turn from his former ways.

SURELY THE LORD IS IN THIS PLACE

This place Jacob spent the night was at one time called Luz, meaning place of separation or departure. This could not be more true for Jacob. This was his first night away from home. For the first time in his life, his parents were not in the next tent if he needed or wanted them. Matter of fact, running back to the shelter of his mother's apron was not an option. If he did, he might lose his life. No matter what

Jacob faced as he journeyed away from home, it could not be as bad as what lay behind him but that didn't make what might lay ahead of him any less daunting. He was insecure, uncertain of his future and engulfed in pure unadulterated FEAR! What choice did he have? After the stunt he had pulled with his father and his brother Esau, Jacob is forced to be a man and move on, whether he wanted to or not.

Separated from his home and family perhaps permanently, he would now have to handle his own affairs. A man in his seventies by this time, he was forced to reach a place of spiritual puberty. The place formerly known as Luz, or place of separation, he came to know as Bethel, or the *house of God*. Though still quite green spiritually, he had matured enough to recognize the house of God.

Imagine that! This place of total, complete and extreme separation would forever be known to Jacob as the house of God!

LOOKING AFTER GROWN CHILDREN

It was no surprise really, that it took so long and such drastic measures to bring Jacob to a level of maturity. He was used to his mother calling the shots. Surely he wondered how he would survive without her advice and direction. In all likelihood, so did his mother. Could he survive on his own? Would he know what to do without her guidance? The fact that she sent him to her brother Laban may be an indication she still felt he needed to be somewhere he would be looked after. This becomes more evident as we learn more of Laban later.

Sadly, dependence on parents to carry the responsibility of grown children is a common occurrence today. Many grown children are completely dependent upon their parents in decision making and finances. It seems impossible they could make their own way. Years ago women married young and took care of families. Today, many grown children live at home expecting provision from their parents long after they become adults. It is a trap for both parent and child. This trap hinders both parent and child from their God-given destinies, blocking fulfillment of promise and maturity. Do not fall into this trap!

You can waste your life tending to a grown child's needs and wind up with nothing. Sometimes a life-sucking spiritual child will do the same thing. Draw on you until all your time and focus is on their needs. You find yourself afraid they will not go on with God without your prodding and pushing. The feeling that if you don't supply, there will be no supply is a lie, a deception from the enemy of our souls. If God does not keep them, they will not be kept.

It is God's responsibility to supply, for both us and our children. Many times a grown child must be forced to make their own way. Then they often develop a sense of accomplishment from striving to make their own way.

IF GOD WILL BE WITH ME .... SO THAT I GO HOME IN PEACE

Jacob named the place Bethel, or house of God, set up a pillar, and vowed a vow to God. Too bad he was not completely free of his selfish nature and self-serving ambition. Jacob was awestruck and even a bit frightened at the overwhelming dream he had out here all alone but wasn't quite ready to completely commit his way to God without trying to strike a deal.

It was simply Jacob's way. So, Jacob vowed a vow. He says, *"Oh, I've seen where angels travel back and forth from heaven to earth! I've seen God standing up above and He has hand delivered my promise. To God, I'm special! Sure... I'm running for my life from my brother for taking something God promised to give me anyway but God still thinks I'm special. God is still in control. So, God, IF you will be with me, keep me on the way, feed me, clothe me, and bring me back home in peace, THEN you will be my GOD!"* IF He will, THEN I will. Jacob, true to his nature made a vow that was conditional at best. It looks as though Jacob didn't fully trust man or God at the time.

JACOB HAS A HORMONE HURRICANE

Ah, what an encounter! Jacob, with the taste of sweet communion with God in his mouth, continued his journey to Laban's. When he first arrived, he found a well in a field with flocks of sheep by it. Flocks gathered and the men lifted the stone to water the flocks.

As Jacob surveyed his surroundings, he asked about Laban and it was not long after his eyes fell upon Rachel, Laban's daughter, who was about to water her father's sheep. Upon first sight of her, he fell head over heels in love, instantly and completely with young, beautiful Rachel.

Perhaps Jacob was mesmerized by her beauty and forgot himself because it was not long and he began to break the rules. Take your sheep and go on now, he told them. Water the sheep and go and feed them. While he was speaking with them Rachel approached with her father's sheep.

Earlier, they had uncapped the well. It likely took more than one person to uncap it because the Bible says a great stone was on the well's mouth. It was normally a group effort to remove the stone, water the animals and replace the stone but in what must have appeared to be some sort of bizarre mating dance, Jacob uncapped the well for Rachel *all by himself!*

JACOB KISSED RACHEL AND WEPT

Oh how excited Jacob must have been to realize this beautiful young woman was Laban's daughter! Jacob was so moved by Rachel's beauty and his desire for her that in reckless abandon Jacob kissed Rachel, yelled out and wept!

Jacob is accustomed to beautiful women. Sarah, his grandmother, was so beautiful that young men desired her in her old age. His mother Rebekah, was a beautiful woman, therefore, it would take an exceptional beauty to impress Jacob and Rachel is the one! No need for further investigation of the young available women in Padan-Aram, Jacob has found THE one! Rachel is it!

Attempting to restrain his emotions, Jacob drew back to behold her loveliness from a slight distance. As he beheld Rachel, he caught a glimpse of his future and realized the possibility that it could be better than he had originally thought. For a brief moment, he saw that she held his future in her hand. This fleeting glimpse of what "could be" produced a feeling of joy and relief in Jacob's mind.

Relief is a powerful sensation to experience for someone with his nature. Jacob was not accustomed to the intense emotional strain he had been experiencing since that fateful day of deception. He was a man who enjoyed the simple things in life. Jacob's ill-advised decision had complicated his life to the point of bewilderment. Remember, this was a man in his seventies. His life consisted of going to the fields and coming home to a mother who had everything under control. Jacob had no real responsibility or ambition it seemed.

One irresponsible and reckless decision had exposed a conniving and manipulating personality that he may or may not have realized was there. Nevertheless, everything in his life had changed and it was not for the better. At least that is how it seemed, until now!

Now, he has found Rachel. His encounter with Rachel impacted his life in such a profound way that yet another change is inevitable. Finally, it seems there is hope for the future. The glimpse of grandeur caused him to anticipate that a lifestyle of manic manipulation and frantic fleeing might not be his only option. This assignment to Haran seemed to be coming together with little effort on Jacob's part. It was as if the eye of God was guiding him. Was that not exactly what God had promised him at Bethel?

Completely enthralled and enchanted, Jacob had impulsively KISSED Rachel. The earthy fragrance of her windblown hair and the glistening of her bronze tone, sun soaked skin was breathtaking. As he drank in her beauty, Jacob was overwhelmed with desire. This was like a whirlwind. With burning passion commandeering him Jacob endeavors to evaluate this overwhelming desire and gain control of his thoughts. He realizes such familiarity toward and unmarried woman is totally unacceptable. Jacob was not supposed to kiss Rachel. In fact, he was not supposed to even touch her! Here again, Jacob is breaking every rule! Jacob was completely enraptured by Rachel and found himself reeling in a dreamlike state.

This is exactly what we do! When God speaks a word to us, we put faith in overdrive and throw patience and protocol out the window. We do not want to talk patience, we have FAITH! We have had a meeting with God. We journey on running head long into the promise and are feeling invincible. It is breath-taking-exhilirating! It is as if nothing can stop us now! There are no limitations!

We may break all the rules because the word and promise given us is overwhelming! It is so precious and beautiful and means so much to us we find ourselves in a dreamlike state. Unfortunately, we do not always make the best or most mature decisions from that place or in that state.

It seems Jacob might have mentioned to Rachel that he was family *before* he kissed her, but he had broken all the other rules, why do differently now? Jacob had come looking for a wife. He was supposed to find a wife from his people. As far as Jacob was concerned, it was all over except the ceremony.

True to nature, Jacob was making assumptions. How did he know she was not already spoken for? Did he know where she fell in the line of siblings? Would Laban receive him, much less the idea that he had already staked a claim on his daughter? When you are Jacob, such minute principles matter very little.

Are we like Jacob in that we latch on to the first glittery, beautiful, thing we see in an inappropriate manner? Does God mean for us to grab hold of the first word spoken over us? Does he allow us to see it glitter and shimmer to whet our appetite for what He has in store for later? Too often we forge ahead without first considering what may be required of us along the way. What does God have lined up to prepare us for this beautiful future promise? Our perception of what we need or do not need is often formed out of selfish desire and from a limited perspective just as Jacob's was fashioned.

After all, Jacob feels he has walked right into the middle of his destiny! However, all that glitters is not gold. Sometimes the most beautiful and precious things in our lives have not one iota of glitz or glamour. It would be some time before Jacob would come to this realization. Right now, he is flying high! He has escaped certain death at the hands of an angry brother and walked right into the presence of the most beautiful woman he has ever laid eyes on! A win-win situation!

LABAN COMES TO MEET JACOB

Jacob's uncle Laban comes, greets him with a kiss and takes him to his home. Over dinner, Jacob shares intimate details of his situation back home. After all, Laban is family, on his mother's side. Laban will surely understand Jacob's plight. In fact, after he finishes with his pitiful story, he just might be in good enough with Laban that he can get a little closer to Rachel. Both Laban and Jacob are content for him to stay and he is there about a month when the question of a more permanent arrangement arises.

Little did Jacob know at the time, but his egocentric personality traits ran rampant through this family. Laban had Laban's best interest at heart from the beginning. After hearing Jacob's story he undoubtedly realized, Jacob had nowhere else to go. He had burned his bridges and uncle Laban was his last real chance for a normal life. Laban made himself look good and offered job security to Jacob by extending to Jacob the opportunity to determine his own wages. What a guy! Laban seemed benevolent but it would not be long before it was obvious he was manipulating the situation in his favor.

CHAPTER 5

An Uglier Than Ugly Ugliness - Jacob's New Life Goes South

LABAN HAD TWO DAUGHTERS — RACHEL AND LEAH

JACOB WOULD SOON learn that Laban not only fathered beautiful, young Rachel whom he was so smitten with but he also had an older daughter named Leah. Her name means, weary or tired and the Bible says that Leah was tender eyed. Leah had weak or delicate eyes. The truth is Leah was UGLY!

We have already surmised Rachel's beauty and now we realize she is Laban's younger daughter. She was the one Jacob met first and by this time he was madly in love with. Jacob met Rachel first because she was out tending the sheep. Leah's delicate eyes were likely the reason she was not out in the fields. Still, it could very well have been due to the difference in their personalities.

Rachel's name means *sheep*. Rachel appeared strong and hearty but her name tells us that her personality was higher maintenance than was obvious at first glance. Sheep denotes a timid, defenseless creature. Sheep are easily influenced or led astray. We soon see that Rachel will live up to her name.

I WILL SERVE SEVEN YEARS FOR RACHEL

Sheep or no sheep, Jacob was madly in love with Rachel! The only wages he wanted was Rachel's hand in marriage. Jacob knew exactly what he wanted and he was specific about which daughter he desired.

Gen 29:18 "and Jacob loved Rachel and said, I will serve thee seven years for Rachel thy YOUNGER daughter."

Jacob's love for Rachel and serving Laban for seven years with only Rachel as a wage was a noble idea as far as Laban was concerned. At Jacob's request, Laban agreed to give Rachel to him for a wife for his willingness to work for her the appointed time. *Better you than another Jacob.*

Jacob is delighted at the aspect of having such a beautiful and desirable wife so off to work he goes. He works for Rachel seven long years and the Bible tells us it seemed only a few days because of the love he had for her. As he worked, he must have dreamed and yearned for her. Oh the restraint Jacob must have shown as he courted beautiful Rachel. The anticipation and preparation was a great joy for Jacob as he envisioned taking her to his tent and making her his wife. He dreamed of embracing her and never letting go. She would be his bride soon, very soon and well worth it. The promise of Rachel becoming his wife energized and enabled him to easily complete his tasks.

Rachel's beauty soothed his weary mind at night and propelled him forth during the day. Seven years of labor in the heat of Haran but she was worth it. His heart was set and the thought of her consumed him. She was all he longed for. He envisioned them living together and having children that would fulfill the promise given him through his father's blessing and the visitation that frightful night in the wilderness. Never imagining he would desire anything enough to work with energy and excitement for it, Jacob labored in the heat of the day with dedication and expectation. This was a new experience for him! In this dreamlike state, time was no issue.

As the seven-year contract was fulfilled Jacob approached Laban to make good his promise. Laban threw a party and to be perfectly frank they all got drunk. Laban gave his daughter to Jacob. Inebriated and with seven years of expectancy under his belt, Jacob was off to the bedchamber to consummate the union of him and his promised Rachel. Finally, after seven years of longing for this day, he was taking the beauty he had labored for rigorously to his bed.

For seven years Jacob had imagined all that he would say to her on this night. The sweet nothings he intended to whisper in her ear would cause her to know his love for her ran deep like a river. He would tell her how irresistible he had found her to be since that first day when his eyes fell on her. How his devotion for her had enabled him to stay the course. Jacob intended Rachel to realize there had not been one day go by that he had not been captivated and tantalized by her inviting charm. The very thought of her had enticed him. Her engaging warmth and grace fascinated him. He intended her to realize how her beauty had stimulated, captivated and motivated him for seven years. The fires of passion were burning out of control!

Jacob would hold nothing back and with a bottle of wine in his belly, he was all the more daring. Jacob had romanced her in his mind over and over. After this night, he would never again go to his bed alone. He would embrace her and they would forever live together in wedded bliss and the union would produce beautiful children, thereby establishing the covenant God had made with him and his family all the way back to his grandfather.

The custom in that country was for the groom to go to bed first and then the mother of the bride or some near relative to bring the bride to his bedchamber, veiled and in the dark as a sign of purity. The bride was not allowed to speak.

Mind filled with fantasy and his passionate heart about to burst, slightly intoxicated Jacob lay there waiting for his beautiful, promised bride to be presented to him. What promise this night held! All the labor, frustration, aggravation and exasperation now behind him, Jacob's life was about to take on new meaning.

JACOB GIVEN LEAH, THE UGLY SISTER INSTEAD – WAKING UP WITH LEAH

The last seven years had seemed only a few days. There was the feast, the wedding and now it was time to actually be with Rachel, the one and only thing he had truly desired enough to labor for all his life. Jacob had played out this scenario in his mind hundreds of times.

Jacob was convinced he was going to bed with a beauty but little did he know; the deceiver was being deceived! Laban had given his older, ugly daughter Leah as a wife to Jacob. Jacob was anticipating Rachel, his beauty but was about to wake up with Leah. It is difficult to imagine how Jacob could have mistaken one for another but he did. That must have been one dark tent!

The next morning, Jacob awoke with a fright. In the morning light, he discovered Leah. He had gone to bed with a beauty but had awakened with a beast. *It wasn't Rachel at all! It was her older, Ugly sister Leah!*

To the great extent that Rachel was beautiful, Leah was not. Weak eyed, tender eyed, delicate eyed or cross eyed, whatever you want to call it, she was ugly. Her father knew she was ugly, Jacob knew she was ugly and she knew she was ugly. What degree of ugly, if there are degrees, we do not know but Laban must have considered her extremely ugly to feel he had to deceive Jacob, a deceiver himself, in order to find her a husband. Apparently, no one wanted her. At least that was her father's assumption.

Leah was likely a hard-working, strong woman. Short on self-esteem and long on feelings of rejection, she may have worked extra hard to please. Her womanly skills were likely honed and polished and truth is, she probably would make any man a wonderful wife but who would know that? Who would choose her?

Think of the words Leah heard that night. Jacob thought he was with his beloved and long awaited Rachel. Why didn't she say something? It must have broken her heart to hear those passion filled words and know they were not meant for her. After all, she and Jacob were married. What would change if she revealed who she really was? Maybe she was in on this deception or maybe Leah had to keep quiet. Possibly she was a victim as well and had only the hope of one night of love with her new husband before he realized it was ugly Leah and not beautiful Rachel he lay with.

You have to wonder. Where was Rachel in this whole setting? Why did she not come running in to Jacob telling him how her father was deceiving him? How long had she known that Leah was the one who would take her place? Did she care? The Bible talks of Jacob's love for Rachel but what about her love for him? He was, after all in his seventies. Did she expect to marry Jacob at the end of the seven years or had they discussed it? Was she so intimidated by her father that she dare not tell about the switch?

How long did it take Jacob to confront Laban? He confronted him immediately! Laban acknowledged Jacob's grievance by offering a lame excuse about custom. The elder daughter *must* be given in marriage before the younger. Laban does not even try to deny his trickery but passes this offense off as customary. Proof of the custom; there is no proof. Was Laban considering this strategy all along or did he dream it up sometime during the seven years? Laban and Jacob were both deceivers and a deceiver is destined to be deceived.

Jacob had labored for seven years. He fulfilled his contract, with honor. Likely the first time Jacob had ever done such a thing. The number seven represents completion and signifies that the Lord accomplished something in Jacob during that period. Jacob, a man prone to inactivity had made himself a servant to a member of his own family and served with intent and purpose. This completed work prepared him to embark upon the phase of his process that would ultimately escort him into his destiny.

I'LL GIVE YOU RACHEL-FOR SEVEN MORE YEARS

Laban instructed Jacob to fulfill Leah's week, which was seven days of feasting in celebration of the marriage. Then he could have Rachel for his wife also if he were willing to serve seven more years! Laban had no problem allowing Jacob to have Rachel; especially since he had successfully unloaded ugly Leah. *Sure Jacob, I'll give you Rachel, as you desire but as for Leah? Well, she belongs to you too.* Jacob must have been thinking, *Oh great! What a deal!* Sure Jacob was willing to work seven more years for Rachel. Why not? He had to live with ugly Leah anyway. Working for Rachel would give him a way to get out of the house! He was less than excited about his new wife and strangely enough, this former homebody was ready and willing to get back to work! Anything to keep him from going home to that ugly woman Leah!

Laban's lack of regard for Leah's feelings in the matter and his request that Jacob fulfill Leah's week may have pulled ever so slightly at Jacob's heartstrings in sympathy toward her. After all, Jacob knew what it was like to have a father who preferred a sibling. Leah was no prize and everyone knew it but the least Jacob could do was fulfill her week. *You already have Leah. Fulfill her week Jacob and as for Rachel? I'll make you a deal!*

Jacob's love for Rachel was motivation enough for him to embark on *another* seven years of labor. This determination, fortitude and unadulterated grit substantiates his love and yearning for her. The problem? The second seven years had a different slant. The Bible says that the first seven years seemed but a few days, is says nothing of the sort concerning the second seven years and I'm sure we know why. Jacob was living with an ugly woman. Jacob was working for Rachel yes, but every day must have been a reminder that he was tricked by his father in law and living with ugly Leah.

What was it like for Leah during this early period with Jacob? Did he treat her with anger and resentment because of the trickery of her father? Did he make it known he would *never* truly accept her? Maybe Jacob had evolved to the point he was compassionate toward her plight but still she *had* been party to the deception. He may have treated her with indifference simply because she was not his beloved Rachel. Cooking, cleaning and maybe a child or two; she would serve a purpose but she was not Rachel, nor would she ever be.

How Leah must have longed every day for Jacob to hold her the way he did that first night when he thought she was Rachel. She had truly experienced how loving and gentle he could be if his heart was with her. You wonder how he treated her when he came in to her subsequently. Maybe their first night together left such an impression that it brought him to her time and time again throughout their marriage. She undoubtedly tried hard to impress him. Still, the love of his life was beautiful Rachel. He may get used to the idea of Leah but he loved Rachel.

INTRODUCTION OF PROMISE AND PROCESS

By now, we have an understanding that Jacob represents us. Rachel is a representation of the beautiful promise God has given us and Leah? Well, Leah represents the process it takes for us to accomplish the level of integrity guaranteeing we are trustworthy to possess the precious promise.

Rachel was beautiful and well favored but Leah was a constant reminder. To get to Rachel, Jacob had to accept Leah. If he does not embrace Leah now, Rachel will never be a part of his life. He will love, desire and admire Rachel but never have her without the acceptance of ugly Leah. He is working for Leah as well as Rachel and there was no way to forget that!

Likewise, we will never have our beautiful promise without acceptance of an ugly process we want so desperately to ignore. Our promise is desirable, beautiful and truly well favored, but the process? It is difficult at best and just plain UGLY! It gives you no status, prominence, reputation, standing or esteem. It goes against everything you have ever wanted but without embracing it the promise will never be yours to have and to hold. The quicker you accept this, the more rapidly you will experience fulfillment.

PROCESS WILL WEAR ON YOU-IT IS UGLY AND UNEXPECTED

As stated earlier, Leah's name means weary and it is plain to us that she was not much to look. It is the same with the process. Her relationship with Jacob symbolizes the process the Lord issues to each of our lives in order to create the character, integrity and moral fiber needed in order to fulfill the promise.

It probably goes without saying that the process we go through can and often does make us weary. If we do not allow ourselves to grow weary in well doing or faint in our minds, we reap the benefits of the process according to Galatians 6:9.

Reaping benefit is what we long for, is it not? Just as Jacob longed for Rachel, we long for our promise. Just as Rachel was beautiful so it is with our promise but we will soon learn that much greater benefit can be gleaned from the process.

Just as Leah was ugly and her presence unexpected, so is our process.

The methods the Lord uses to produce the characteristics needed to reach our destiny and realize the promise are many times unexpected and ugly. Imagine spending every minute of every day tied to someone or something you do not want; forced to live with something you were tricked into. That was Jacob's dilemma. You see, his promise, Rachel was present, but she proved to be a package deal. Beautiful Rachel came with an ugly sister. It might not have been so bad if she were an unsightly lamp or a hideous figurine you could hide away in a closet and never look at. There is a lot to be said for out of sight out of mind. This was not the case with Leah. Leah was a living, breathing reminder that the deceiver had been deceived.

How angry Jacob must have been at Laban, at Leah, at the entire situation. Oh, the reminder Leah must have been of the trickery of his father in law. What a reminder of the mistakes he had made. You have to wonder if he ever thought of how he tricked his brother Esau into selling his birthright or of his father Isaac as he remembered how he had deceived him to attain the blessing.

Rachel was one thing in Jacob's life he tried to attain honestly and look what happened. Not only did he wind up with the wrong girl, he wound up with the *ugly* one! It must have been difficult to face Leah every day. *Jacob* knew he had not chosen Leah. *Rachel*, Jacob's beloved, the one he adored and wanted to devote to completely knew he had not chosen Leah. *Laban* knew he had not chosen Leah but most of all, *Leah* knew Jacob had not chosen Leah. Nonetheless, he would have to share his estate, his wealth and even his bed with this ugly woman.

The sheer obligation he must have felt. It was obvious to everyone her dance card would never be full. How could he completely reject her? There were sobering moments when he felt badly for her. After all, this was not what any of them bargained for, except maybe Laban. Laban found his ugly daughter Leah a husband, as well as Rachel and had Jacob working his fingers to the bone for nearly nothing. What more could Laban want? What was Jacob to do? He was not one who dealt well with confrontation. He would do whatever it took to keep peace but the charge was colossal.

UGLY NEVER OCCURS TO US WHEN GOD IS INVOLVED

We are creatures who love beauty and ease. We willingly wear ourselves out attempting to attain it. Every young man dreams of marrying a beautiful young woman. He does not fancy he will wind up with an ugly hag. Every young woman longs to find her prince charming.

We see the promise God has given us, and we find it is magnificent! We enjoy feasting our eyes and focusing our thoughts on it but the process, not so much. When God speaks a beautiful, inspiring word to us, it never enters our minds our path might be sprinkled with difficulty much less inundated with ugly!

So it goes with us as we journey through the process. Something within wants to believe we should walk into God's beautiful purpose for our lives unscathed and untouched by ugly. This type of thinking is simply unrealistic. It quickly fosters discouragement. Entitlement thinking hinders and immobilizes us rather than helping us to progress.

The process is very rarely lovely. Leah, representing process was ugly and not what Jacob desired. The process we live with is equally as daunting and every bit as ugly; not what we bargained for. The unsightliness of the process is ever before us. It reminds us of skewed plans and an inability to protect ourselves from undesirable circumstances. It highlights the humanity that is our makeup, a part of us we would rather no one ever see. It exposes even more character flaws than we were aware were possible. We are self-aware regarding generalized flaws but the process will yank the covers and expose us completely.

What mistakes have you made; what regrettable choices? Did you make a million mistakes only to realize just when you thought you had it right, there was mistake one million and one? The process exposes and corrects. It can be hideous but necessary. The end result is peaceable fruits of righteousness. The process will facilitate the promise of God, no matter what it looks like.

Jacob, the deceiver, found himself on the receiving end of deception with his new father-in-law. Though Jacob was devastated regarding Laban's duplicity regarding Leah, this would prove to be only the beginning. The process would be lengthy and tiresome and Jacob would be subjected to enough deceitfulness to cause him to reconsider his wayward ways. Often times that is all it takes to locate us as well. When we come face to face with our own tactics we see things differently. It is then that we begin to make necessary adjustments.

CHAPTER **6**

The Ugly Woman And Her Beautiful Fruit

LORD SAW LEAH WAS HATED – OPENED HER WOMB

WHAT WOULD HAVE happened if Jacob had graciously accepted Leah as the gift from God she was? Maybe she wasn't beautiful on the outside but before Jacob reached the end of his life, he would begin to recognize the beautiful purpose she had served. At this time though, Leah is hated. And when God saw how hated she was, He opened her womb. The beautiful Rachel though, was barren.

Jacob was not ready or willing to accept the process which God chose to develop his character. He preferred Rachel. Of course he did. Rachel was beautiful, younger and the one Jacob chose for himself. She embodied every beautiful thing he could imagine for his future. All those years he had labored for her, hoping, dreaming, and expecting a perfect beautiful life to come out of their union.

Remember, God visited him. His life changed from that point. God told him He would be with him, guide him and He did, straight to Rachel. The thing Jacob did not want to accept was that God also led him straight to Leah. God lead Jacob straight into the process that would perfect him and propel him into the blessing. The trickery of Laban, being saddled with the ugly sister, having to work seven more years for a man he must have resented; none of this was part of the deal.

From our perspective, it is easy to see the positive contribution Leah made in Jacob's life. From Jacob's perspective it seemed like excess baggage. Leah though, was in a hard place, a furnace of affliction so to speak.

Is there an ugly process in your life that seems to be interfering with your promise? Of course there is. The two are inseparable. Read your Bible from cover to cover and you will find countless situations where the process and the promise reside together. Is it pleasant? Is it your first choice? Is it any choice you would *ever* make? No! That is only because you cannot see the big picture. God has control. It is, after all, his plan.

Isaiah 48:10 says *behold I have refined thee, but not with silver, I have chosen thee in the furnace of affliction.* God knows where you are. We do not have a Savior who is unable to understand our suffering. The desperation we feel, the hopelessness we experience is not missed by Him. Our heart cries are not without an ear to hear. Our questions do not float out into the universe unanswered. God does not scoff at our pain. The dead silence we feel surrounded by is not thick enough to keep our Lord at bay. What looks like a hopeless situation is simply the instrument He has chosen to show himself mighty through you.

Leah could do nothing about her situation in her own strength. She was not a bad person, she could not help how she looked, nor could she control whether or not she was loved. She could only control her response to the situation.

God was the one who would come through for Leah; and so He did. He did not deliver Leah out of an unloving relationship. He did not cause her husband to fall madly in love with her regardless of her looks. God can do anything. He could have caused her looks to change or caused Jacob to view her differently but He did not.

God's way of helping Leah; He opened her womb. He made her productive. In fact, He made her extremely productive. She not only bore children, she bore Jacob sons. Was Jacob disgusted when he had to sleep with her? Was it out of duty or pity? We will never know for sure but for whatever reason, he did come in to her and God blessed the occasion. She became undeniably indispensable to his blessing, his future. She, the ugly one, the hated one, the unwanted one was the one who gave birth to the firstborn son of the promise carrying grandson of Abraham. It was her children who would help mature Jacob into the promise carrying patriarch God said he was.

Leah had likely been in the furnace of affliction most of her life. Still, Jacob should have been accepting of the ugly woman of process as an intricate part of God's plan. It would have made things easier for Leah but instead, God stepped in. Jacob had chosen Rachel but God had chosen Leah. In this place of discomfort, God blessed Leah with an open womb. In the east during this period, this was her validation. Value was placed on a woman according to her ability to bare children. Barrenness was a curse but an open womb, meant God was smiling on Leah whether Jacob was or not. Hopefully, this would help in her relationship with him as well.

Leah knew to do one thing. In her furnace of affliction, she knew to call on God. We will see this more clearly as we delve into the names and natures of each child she bore in that furnace and under affliction. She bore beautiful fruit while there and we will soon see that we could learn a lesson or two from the graceful way this ugly woman conducted herself.

THE GIFT-LEAH HAS REUBEN – NOW HE WILL LOVE ME!

Out of a furnace of affliction Leah began to produce fruit and the fruit she produced was good. Leah bore Jacob a son and named him Reuben. He was Jacob's firstborn and his name meant *a gift from God.*

The child and his name were significant in that he was the first of several tools in a spiritual arsenal God was preparing to bring Jacob into the promise. For Leah, Reuben was a gift that might help her to find favor with her husband. When Leah bore Reuben she said, *now my husband will love me!*

Leah knew what kind of predicament she was in. It was not illogical to hope this gift, this son would substantiate her in Jacob's eyes. A beautiful son! What greater blessing could Leah receive? Jacob could not deny the presence of this lovely child and desire to see him would surely bring Jacob all the closer to Leah's tent. Having children, especially sons meant everything to a woman during that time. The score was one for the ugly wife and zero for the beautiful wife. Having the firstborn *son* was like hitting a home run!

There is no recorded response from Jacob regarding the child. If having this beautiful gift made any difference to Jacob at all it is not known. As far as we can tell, the child brought no special favor to Leah. It seemed Jacob only had eyes for Rachel. His focus was on her beauty and what their future might hold. Even though their future appeared to be of his beloved Rachel sitting in her tent, looking beautiful and nothing more! At this juncture, for Jacob, that was enough!

For us, Reuben, the firstborn son represents the gifting God places within each of us. Neither Jacob, nor Leah realized the impact this child would have in their lives. Like them, we are often unmindful of how our gift affects our spiritual future.

God has placed in each of us, a special gift to be used in the life he has preordained. Our gift is part of the process that leads us to the promise. We have a gift that comes with the call of God. Our individual gift is precious to us. It becomes as precious as a firstborn son to a mother, especially an ugly, hated mother.

Reuben was Jacob's gift but Jacob failed to realize how instrumental this gift was. Had he stopped for a moment to embrace the gift and consider how it might be part of God's plan for his future, things might have been quite different. If he took pause at this beautiful gift, we do not see evidence. At this time, it seemed Jacob's focus was on dreams of building a family with beautiful Rachel. The children born out of his forced union with Leah were simply a bi-product.

❧❧❧

Like Jacob, we fail to realize the potential and purpose in our gift. In spiritual circles we hear about spiritual gifting, super-natural gifts, etc. Yet few have real understanding of the gift. We are spiritually gifted, we are naturally gifted. Both are for the purpose of God's glory and a part of the process that leads us to the promise. The anointed of God, who experience real relationship with Him usually experience success in many things. They are proficient in more than one endeavor but usually, one thing or another stands out.

When you see someone prosperous at most anything they attempt, you will find many opinions. There will be naysayers, encourages, skeptics. Many times you will hear another Christians say *this is your call, your gift, you must do this one thing to the glory of God!* True, we should use our gifts for God's glory but use caution and realize the anointing of God upon us. As His children we carry with us many strengths and abilities. As we strive to glorify Him with our lives, we may be quite successful at even the smallest of undertakings. Attempting to do everything we find ourselves successful in and calling it *our gift*, can cause us to veer off the path and become distracted, stressed out and ineffective.

Be patient. Your gift will reveal itself. It will stand out. Your gift will draw you like a moth to a flame even if you attempt to reject it. The thing that we want to cultivate the least, the thing that seems the most difficult to bring into focus and discipline is often what we can safely call the *gift*.

You see, Jacob wanted sons and he *knew* what a gift a son was but he wanted a son from Rachel, not Leah. So, inadvertently, he was rejecting the gift God gave him. This child was the beginning of the innumerable seed God had promised Jacob. He was an instrumental piece in fulfillment of God's covenant with Jacob, his father and his grandfather. Yet, Jacob appeared not to notice.

This blatant inattention was only a first but would prove to be a neglectful thread that ran through Jacob in the early years with his new family. Rather than embrace what was the beginning of the process God had planned all along, Jacob simply ignored it and went on his way, focusing on what he perceived God had for him; Rachel.

Sometimes our gifting surfaces before we are mature enough to understand it. It may catch us by surprise that God, the creator of the universe would choose us. Why would He place something so precious within such a frail structure? After all, He knows every character flaw and personality defect. He is aware of every bad choice we have ever made. Yet He places within us a great gift or ability.

Why would God do this? Being cognizant of each right and wrong decision and our great potential to continue making them, God still takes a chance on us. Remember? He is a sovereign God. He sees the end from the beginning. He created us exactly as we are. He knows what he is getting into. He knows exactly what gift to place in us to bring us to the promise.

It cannot help but streamline our process if we refuse to follow Jacob's example of ignoring the process. We have the opportunity to accept and embrace the gift even when it comes from somewhere unexpected or undesirable. Granted, it can be difficult to understand how this one small ability could lead us to the promise when it appears to be coming from the opposite direction but it can.

Though we feel open and receptive to God, we are quite short-sighted when it comes to His plan for us. Our best attempt to understand how one unrefined ability could help lead us into the promise falls terribly short. With a mouth filled with prayer and an ear tuned to hearing and arms willing to embrace even what we do not understand, we become students. We learn, when properly applied and disciplined, our gift carries the potential to effect change on not only our little circle of friends and family but the world around us!

God does not shrink back from using us. Sadly, we are the ones adversely moved by mistakes and mishaps in our past. God knew what choices we would make. He knew our actions and reactions. Yet He continues unmoved. He does not call a halt to the covenant promise He has given us, running back to the drawing board to recreate a better, faster, stronger you or me. The Bible tells us that God does not change his mind. Romans 11:29 says, *the gifts and calling of God are without repentance.* News flash! *We were specifically designed for the job!*

The Bible also tells us in Proverbs 18:16 that *a man's gift makes room for him and brings him before great men.* Our gift propels us forward. It inspires us to move ahead and has the ability to produce excellence and bring honor. Our gift can create smoothness and ease in areas where others find it nearly impossible to excel.

CANNOT PLACE CONFIDENCE IN GIFT

It is important also to remember, our gift is not the whole. It is one factor that in the sum of the whole. It is an instrumental part of the process that will bring forth the promise of God and fulfill his covenant with us. Still, it is only a *part.*

The gift of God enables us to do and do with great success. You may be gifted in effective communication, counseling, or simply one on one conversation. You may put pen to paper and produce copy that melts the heart of the most hardened sinner. You may sing like a bird and bring thousands of lost souls to the altar. Whatever your gift you will find you cannot place your full trust and confidence in the gift. You may captivate an audience with an anointed voice that pierces the very soul of mankind yet that gift can and will fail you if you misplace your trust.

When the gift reveals itself, it is easy to feel validated. The problem is, as it was with Leah, this kind of thinking is a false affirmation. Leah's firstborn, Reuben was a beautiful gift for a hated, unloved woman and his presence could not be denied by anyone involved. Her hope was that Jacob would now love her. Reuben's birth solicited little response from his father and in later years he would prove to be unstable, unreliable and untrustworthy. Reuben, the man; would be the picture of loyalty *and* the quintessence of betrayal. He excelled but was unstable and needed containment. He was unpredictable, yet important and instrumental in both process and promise.

Our gift is unstable as well. Placing complete trust in it as though it is the entire package is a huge mistake. Although we cannot rely on the gift alone to bring covenant fulfillment, we can trust it is a necessary part of the process that will lead us to the promise. Like Reuben, our gift is intended to be instrumental in both process and promise.

THE HEARING - LEAH HAS SIMEON - BECAUSE THE LORD HATH HEARD

Jacob's reaction to Reuben was apparently not exactly what Leah had anticipated but all hope was not lost. The Bible says he came in to her and *she conceived again, and bare a son.* Leah saw that the Lord recognized her condition and because of it, gave her this son also. Leah had spent time crying out to God and *God heard,* so she named the child Simeon meaning, *God has heard* or *hears.*

GOD HEARS US

In the midst of the process is it imperative we learn not only to tune *our* ear to hear God but to understand He hears us as well. This is a huge step in maturity and development. Simply because there is zero visibility at the moment does not mean God is not listening. God was with Job. God was with Noah, David and John the Baptist! Each name spoken brings a vision of each individual's moments of crisis but with our vantage point we understand God was present.

Leah was a woman who knew about process. She was a woman who called on God in her affliction more than once and had the assurance He would hear and answer. The children she bore and the names she gave them are the evidence.

Part of the process is learning that in times of affliction we should not focus on the pain or impossibility of the situation. We must learn to call on God and understand that He always hears. We should always be listening for His voice.

Leah was putting all her eggs in one bassinette, so to speak. She could not change one thing regarding her circumstances. Leah could not change her looks. Nothing would dampen Jacob's desire for Rachel. Therefore, appealing to him was pointless. He had worked fourteen years without question to have Rachel as his wife. He did not willingly work one day for Leah. Had she appealed to Jacob as her source of help, it would have been misplaced and misguided.

Where did she turn? She went to God and God heard. He heard when she bore Reuben, the firstborn son of Jacob and heard yet again when he gave her Simeon, the second son. Her circumstances were terrible. Her security those circumstances would be made right? God.

Jacob certainly needed to realize God could change his situation as well. He had forever looked to others to meet his needs and take care of him. Sometimes we are guilty of behaving like Jacob. We exhibit

Jacob's traits often without recognizing it. We always want someone else's spiritual advice, encouragement, consent, ideas, knowledge, prophetic word. We feel we have no answer without an answer from the mouth of another human being. We lean on others to pray yet have little confidence in our own prayers. Who, more than you can understand how to pray for the situations you face? Who, more than you can understand the call of God on your life? Who, besides you, can hear what God is saying to *you*?

Go directly to the source. Approach the throne *boldly*, the bible tells us! Leah knew her source. Why? Because He was her *only* option. Who was looking out for Leah? Who believed in her dream, her vision, her destiny, her promise? No one. Her father simply wanted to pawn her off on some man. Her husband hated her because she was tied to the twisted trickery of her father. Jacob wanted only her beautiful sister. Rachel was so self-absorbed it's doubtful she thought much about Leah at all. At least, that is, until the children started arriving.

Who are you? Are you Jacob? Still running from place to place, expecting a word or sign to get you to the next spiritual position? Do all your dreams and the call of God on your life depend on another pulling the strings? Are you so enamored and star struck by the Word of promise that you fail to see the instruments and circumstances God is using to prepare you for that promise?

Or are you Leah? So hated and rejected that God is the only source you have? Have you been through so much in your lifetime that you understand, if God does not intervene, it is not happening? Have you faced so many devils and so much torment that your only option is to proceed, slow and steady, accepting what comes? Believing beyond belief that God is in control?

There are a lot of people who constantly talk about what the Lord has said to them but they do not seem to do much with those words. Have they really heard God or are they simply hearing themselves? John

10:27 says *My sheep know my voice.* As we begin to truly *hear* God, we become intimate with him. Then, hearing His voice is unmistakable but it is not enough to *hear* God. Those who only hear will become weak because it is the *doing* of the Word of God that builds our faith and spiritual stamina. To be hearers of the word and not doers of the word causes a deception to take place in one's life that is detrimental.

We have *heard* God regarding the promise, without a doubt. We know that we know God has a plan for us. We know God has heard our heart's cry. The problem is we sometimes place too much empha-sis on what we have heard. When God speaks to us we feel strong and empowered. Hearing God and hanging on to that word carries us through hard and troublesome times.

Still, hearing is not the entire package. Our hearing can become dull. Not God's hearing us, of course but our hearing God. There is a bless-ing on the hearer but we must be careful not to be hearers only. Hear-ing is an important part of the process but hearing can fail us. The process is difficult and we cannot allow our hearts to become hard during this time. If we harden our hearts Psalm 95:8 says *we will not, cannot hear God.*

Mark 4:9 says *He that hath ears to hear, let him hear.* We cannot al-low ourselves to become dull of hearting. We must *act on* what we hear the Lord say and it takes discipline and integrity to do so.

THE ADHERANCE, ANOINTING, INTERCESSION-LEAH HAS LEVI

AT LAST MY HUSBAND WILL BECOME ATTACHED TO ME!

Upon yet another son's arrival, Leah believed in her heart that *now* Jacob would be joined to her. So, she called him Levi, meaning to adhere or be joined together. Levi also means priestly anointing or intercession. This child represents the priestly anointing; the anointing to stand before God on behalf of the people and before people on behalf of God. In a sense, Leah must have thought Levi would be the one to bridge the gap between her and her husband.

By now, there are three sons with names meaning gift, hearing and now anointing/intercession. It may seem logical that Rachel, the representative of the promise should have given birth to these sons but no. As of yet, Rachel is not bearing. She remains present and looking quite beautiful. She still dominates Jacob's thoughts and plans. Yet, she has borne him no fruit!

Meanwhile, the beautiful fruit of the process is multiplying rapidly. It was Leah who produced the priestly anointing and ability to bridge the gap between the mistakes of the past and the hope of the future. It was Leah, the hated one, the ugly one, the very thing that was most difficult for Jacob to accept that was giving him the tools he needed to realize the promise.

Likewise, it is what we deem the ugliest and most unacceptable that bears the most fruit in our lives. It is that terrible situation that affords us the empathy to make intercession for another. Have we suffered moral failure, financial devastation or death of a loved one? Have we failed miserably or suffered terribly? Leah did and she produced an anointing, an adherence and an ability to intercede. She called him Levi.

Let me be clear. Suffering is not a requirement for us to make intercession for others. Our intercession can be out of sympathy, empathy or simply out of obedience to God. Sometimes though, we find ourselves paralyzed in pain and forgetting God always provides a way to turn it around and use it for good.

WE MUST BE JOINED TO GOD

We learn while walking through the process no matter how ugly, that we must be joined only to God and His will for us. Jacob still seems unaware that Leah, the ugly woman is bearing beautiful fruit. Rachel the favored one is looking beautiful but making Jacob and the rest of the household miserable.

While our ugly, yet productive process is bearing fruit, we often miss the beauty of it. Our eyes are focused on what we believe holds the importance, the promise. We look at, love, nurture and refuse to take our eyes off of the promise. We think this is exactly what we are supposed to do. We focus on the beauty and shun the ugly, obligatory, mundane, hurtful or tragic. In this, we are missing the real beauty. The ugly process is producing beautiful fruit and is the very thing validating and confirming but we barely notice or outright reject it.

Children were extremely important during this time and were quite important with regard to the promised blessing bestowed on Jacob. How could he not take notice of Leah's fruitful womb? In some way he must have acknowledged within himself. After all, he continued to go in to her and produce these children. We can only speculate what type of relationship may have been developing during this time.

As of yet, Rachel has borne no children and Leah has given Jacob *three* sons! According to Leah, this should count for a great deal but Jacob is still obviously without understanding. The process propelling Jacob to fulfillment of the promise is not yet complete. His desire is still for Rachel even though she has produced nothing. Surely there is a seed somewhere deep within Jacob sprouting into appreciation for this solid, hardworking, enduring, productive though ugly process he calls Leah.

It appears Rachel will never give Jacob children. She is Jacob's choice, the one he desires. He would never have chosen Leah, ever. Yet the beautiful one is not living up to her beauty. Still, it seemed Jacob barely noticed. He only had eyes for Rachel. No doubt the pity at her barrenness endeared him to her more.

There comes a time when we too notice the promise is not producing.

Not to say it never will but there is more at work here than we recognize. The beautiful promise it seems is overshadowed by the very thing we hate. It seems the ugly things we are experiencing are sucking the air in the room and our beautiful promise being suffocated. Patience my friend. . . it's all part of the process.

THE PRAISE-LEAH HAS JUDAH - THIS TIME I WILL PRAISE THE LORD!

Jacob seems to be a bit hard headed. He apparently does not see the direction God really wants for his life. It is obvious to Leah as reflected in the naming of her children and should be to Jacob whom God has chosen and on some level, Jacob gets it. He realizes his Rachel, his beautiful promise plays a huge role in the blessing but he fails to realize she is not all-encompassing.

In the meantime, Leah decides it is time to forget trying to win Jacob's heart and simply *"praise the Lord".* Therefore she names her fourth son Judah, meaning praise. Leah would celebrate *another* son! If Jacob still failed to see Leah's value, it was not because she was a bad or ugly wife and mother. It was because Jacob wore blinders!

Leah made a decision: She would praise God anyway! Leah had come to a pivotal moment. She knew at this point, *It isn't about you Jacob! For years my focus was on how to get your love and attention. How do I make you love me? How do I make you accept me? What will make you stay with me? If I have enough sons, maybe, just maybe you will feel about me the way you feel about Rachel! But it no longer matters! It's no longer about you, nor is it about me. It is about what God has given me and how he is using me. It was God who gave me Reuben, my gift. It was God who gave me Simeon, the ability to hear. Even if you haven't heard my cry, God has. It was God who gave me Levi, the priestly anointing, the ability to intercede and it is God who has now given me Judah, the ability to praise Him. No matter what my relationship with you becomes. I can praise Him because the relationship I have with HIM is worth far more than my relationship with another!*

Leah had found a place of praise we should all recognize but few seem to, especially at first. This is the kind of praise that you reach as far down in you as possible and begin to pull up praise from your innermost being, strictly for the goodness and glory of God. A praise that arises for all he has been and all he has done for you and through you, no matter the circumstances. This praise comes from deep, deep within; a praise that causes you to forget what you have been through and also causes you to forget what you are going through. Leah is going to need this praise because things have only begun to get rocky.

When Leah bore Judah, she already had three other sons. God had been very good to her. *No, I don't have the support and love of my husband but look what the Lord has done for me! God has been good. I will praise the Lord just because I want to. For years I have struggled with a husband who does not love me, a mouthy competitive, high-maintenance sister who shares my husband and the only good things out of this ugly situation are my four beautiful boys. I'm tired of the competition, the struggle, the agony every time I look into Jacob's eyes and realize he does not reciprocate. Someone must evolve and it will be me. I have children. I am blessed. That is more of a future than I had expected to have in my father's house. I will praise the Lord for what I have.* Psalm 116:12 says, *What shall I render unto the Lord for all his benefits toward me?* Leah rendered praise. We should follow her example.

Are you at a place where you have realized it may never work out exactly as you'd hoped it would? We may not understand our circumstances but there is power in our praise. If we have God's approval, then man's approval does not seem quite as important. He really is the only one with our best interest at heart.

Leah, until now, had named each child reflecting hope that she would gain Jacobs favor. Now, she is strictly looking to the Lord. She did not mention Jacob as she named Judah. She only mentioned God.

What a long time it can take for us to find this place in our journey. We may be surrounded by the most difficult or the most precious people but when it comes down to it, it is us and God. His approval and love are to be desired and sought after. It took a while for Leah to come to that realization. She bore three children and practically begged her husband to love and accept her. Think of the trouble between her and her sister. Think of the labor pains she likely bore alone. Think of the agony she'd suffered hoping and dreaming it would all work out before she came to that place of praise.

What an experience; the process I mean. Who feels like praising when the world is caving in on you? Who wants to praise God when the path you are on leads continually through the furnace of affliction, after affliction, after affliction? No one, because we are too busy waiting to *feel* like praising God and *feeling* like it has nothing to do with truly praising God!

Jacob felt like having Rachel for his wife and he had her but that did not make her produce children. He felt like spending more time with Rachel than with Leah but that did not bring about the family he desired with her. Rachel's ability to produce was not within Jacob's power no matter what he felt. Nor did his lack of acceptance of Leah prevent her from producing.

Jacob was a slow learner. Are we? We should not be. The decision lies with us. We may be unhappy with the process God has chosen for us but it is certainly the most productive thing going on in our lives! Our process has produced our gifting, ability to hear and be heard, anointing, intercession, a good dose of stick-to-it-iveness and most of all it produces *praise* in us if we allow it to.

The realization of the gift of God in our life made us want to forge ahead into everything God had in store for us. Hearing God speak to us and having the security he hears us is a source of strength and comfort to us as we move ahead. Standing in the gap for others operating under the anointing is progress in the direction of our destiny. The culmination of all these should produce a powerful, productive, prolific, *PRAISE* regardless of circumstance!

Again, it seems such precious fruit would come from the beautiful one but not so. The promise may be beautiful and we may be grateful for it but it does not produce that type of praise in us. It is the ugly woman who is the mother of this beautiful child! It is the ugliness of the process that brings us to a place where praise resides and abides. Is it not amazing that ugliness can produce such beautiful children? It is what we learn through the ugliness that is productive. It is truly a work God performs! He takes spiritually disfigured and defective people and creates such beautiful, healthy, productive offspring!

Although Judah was not the firstborn of Jacob's children, he soon came to be considered as the chief of Jacob's children. The tribe produced from the ugly woman's child called Judah would become the most powerful and numerous of all of Jacob's children later.

When God chooses you, you prevail. You succeed and find divine favor. When God chooses you, you may be praised by others but more importantly, you learn to praise God! You make a decision within yourself to praise God regardless, as Leah did. When the realization comes that you are not the one in control and your input only stands to make matters worse, just begin to praise Him. It is at that point God steps in and elevates you to the top or ushers you to the front. If God is for you, who can be against you?

As stated earlier but bears repeating, praise God until you forget what you have been through and praise Him until you forget what you are going through.

PART 3:

NOT SO PRETTY UNDER PRESSURE

CHAPTER 7

The Pressure of the Promise - When Nothing Is Happening

DOES JACOB KNOW WHAT HE HAS?

SUDDENLY, EVERYTHING GETS quiet. Jacob has his beloved Rachel. He also has her ugly older sister Leah who he was tricked into marrying by their father Laban and four young sons. You have to wonder if Jacob was even close to seeing the big picture. The life and family he had was not a bad life but not exactly what Jacob had envisioned either.

Jacob, who started out a homeless man with nothing but the clothes on his back has acquired much more than he may realize at this juncture. We can easily see from our perspective that he is developing an arsenal of tools, a foundation of family to support the covenant.

By way of the ugly woman's womb, God has given Jacob much. Firstly, he acquired children who were promised seed that would multiply into an innumerable people. They were the tangible evidence of the covenant God held with Jacob's family for generations. It was the living, breathing, walking, talking evidence of the faith of Abraham.

The events of Jacob's life give hope to the promise God has spoken to us. There is Jacob's firstborn son Reuben, representative of the gift of God. Then there is Simeon, a representative of hearing, acknowledgement and perseverance; a sign that we hear God and just as importantly God hears us. Then we have Levi, who represents the priestly anointing and intercession and we also have Judah, a representative of praise to God in spite of circumstances.

For now, it seems things have settled down in Jacob's family. Rachel has still not conceived. Leah, it appears has stopped bearing. You have to wonder as Jacob faced each day whether or not he thought of home, his early decisions and the place he found himself now. Jacob's promise has yet to produce anything. The process has gone silent. So what now?

WHAT HAPPENS NOW?

Leah we find in a good place. Her acceptance and determination to praise God in spite of circumstances gives her peace and quiet. It seems that same silence is deafening for Rachel.

Now that things have settled in Leah's tent, Rachel begins to cry out for attention yet again. The focus shifts again to the beautiful promise and its underbelly. The promise's inability to produce brings an unsettled, uneasiness and strain on this family.

We, like Jacob, love our Rachel, the promise and hate our Leah, the process. The only redeeming quality the process holds is the hope in its ability to bear fruit in our lives. Like Jacob we often fail to see what it produces as anything but unsolicited and undesirable. We remain sadly unaware of its true value. It is only after time, experience and many tears that we begin to see worth in the suffering and experiences we have long sought to avoid.

Jacob didn't fully understand what God was doing in his life either.

He only knew that for a moment it was quiet. Then suddenly he finds reality bearing down hard on him, again. The barrenness of Rachel was hanging over his head and this beautiful young thing was beginning to pressure him. The fact that Leah had already borne four sons for Jacob was a sore spot to Rachel. In her distress she began to cry out with expectation that Jacob should somehow correct the situation. Rachel could not bear the thought that Leah had not only children but sons and she had nothing. Suddenly, this was issue number one around the dinner table.

YOUR PROMISE CRIES OUT TOO

Do not think your promise is not crying out against the process God has orchestrated in your life as well. It will. It does. It is. Your promise is so alive, so full of power, so real that the mere thought of it illuminates the perceived shortcomings of the process without trying. It's not enough that the process is ugly and undesirable. It seems to be showing up the promise in some sort of unseen competition. The promise is so appealing in its beauty and potential that at its worst we still give it preference over the process.

As we experience seasons in our lives, careers, churches, ministries and relationships, the desire for the promise to produce is weighty. When we do not see results within the perimeters of our expectation, the self-talk begins and we begin to say, *I have produced nothing and likely will produce nothing. Something has to happen and fast! Time is running out!* We begin to question, *where is God? Why isn't something happening? Has he forgotten me?*

Does our paralyzing panic escape God's watchful eye? No, God watches as we begin to squirm under pressure. He is not compelled to remove it or move because of it. He's often silent during this period. The silence seems to come at the worst time but it is through these uncomfortable, pressing times that the process is perfected and the promise undergirded. Though it was not clearly evident in Jacob's situation, it was the same. It was not time for Jacob's beautiful promise to bear fruit and with God, timing is everything.

As parents, we sometimes sit back and let our children make their own decisions, knowing full well they have no real understanding of what choices to make. We allow them to learn lessons and problem solve which fosters maturity in them. God wants us to mature spiritually as well. He often sits quietly watching and waiting, as we work through the process, allowing the promise to hang over our heads, unproductive, at least for a season.

You can almost imagine God's words as He gently says, *So you hate the process I'm taking you through? It is copious and bountiful in ways that make you cringe, yet the beautiful thing you love and desire appears inadequate and cries out for validation. Yes, I'd say this is exactly according to My plan.*

GIVE ME CHILDREN ELSE I DIE

The fact that NOTHING is happening highlights Rachel's inability to produce children. She turns up the heat on Jacob as if her barrenness is somehow his fault.

Envy of Leah gets the better of his beloved and she begins to cry out. *I'm not fruitful! Can't you do something to make me have children? Can you call someone, have a meeting, generate a plan, form a committee that will help me produce sweet baby boys like my ugly sister Leah? Please! I must have children!* Oh, the frustration! Genesis 30:1 says clearly. Rachel became jealous of her sister and said to Jacob, *"Give me children or I'll die!"*

Rachel, Jacob's beloved, beautiful Rachel is in agony! The promise cries out. Yet God remains silent.

How emotionally distressing her barrenness, especially since we know that motherhood was a measuring stick of sorts for a woman at that time. It actually substantiated a woman bestowing a high degree of honor on her yet here was Rachel, empty handed. Rachel is beautiful and if love had anything to do with it, she would have produced a dozen children by now but what does love have to do with it? As much as Jacob loved her, she remained barren.

Though she would not actually die without the validation of children, she felt as though she would. It was a vexation to her and became a point of contention and exasperation to Jacob. Before long, Jacob grew tired of hearing her complaints.

AM I GOD?

Jacob's no drama preference of lifestyle was challenged once again as Rachel pressured him about her desire for children. Be careful what you pray for may have been Jacob's thought as he reflected on his marriage to this beautiful, barren, high-maintenance woman. Jacob had in fact obtained the object of his desire and she was as beautiful as he could ever hope for but her barrenness has become a source of great pressure and we know Jacob is not partial to pressure of any kind.

This extreme strain was enough to kindle Jacob's anger against the one he loved the most. No one need remind him what it meant for Rachel to be barren. No one need tell him the social stigma or the spiritual implications of her barrenness. How could it be that the one he loved the most was cursed with an empty womb? How could a man with promise hanging over him be haunted by the same trouble his parents and grandparents faced?

What was he to do? His grandfather, Abraham had been lured into a maniacal scheme to bear a child through an Egyptian slave girl. He wound up with a house full of trouble. When his mother Rebekah experienced a time of barrenness, his father Isaac, not wanting to repeat his father's mistakes, sought the Lord and pleaded with God to give them a child. Maybe Jacob should have chosen to inquire of God as to why his beautiful Rachel was not producing. Instead the pressure she placed on him began to take its toll.

Rachel's whining and complaining was relentless. The envy she had allowed to occupy her thoughts was unbearable for her and likely made her continual complaints intolerable for Jacob. Jacob's frustration is evident as he becomes offended and challenges Rachel. Jacob bellows, *"Am I in the place of God who has kept you from having children?"* Genesis 30:2 NIV

Jacob knew that only *God* could cause Rachel to bear children. Looking good was not enough. Loving her and doting on her was not enough. Suddenly what looked right and beautiful, the very thing that felt so good and brought him much joy is a source of irritation. The beautiful thing is adding unwanted pressure to an already tedious situation.

I'm not God, Rachel! This is not my fault. It's up to God! What can I do? The pressure escalates to the breaking point. While in Jacob's house and in his grasp, all Rachel has done thus far is look good. She has not produced children but the one thing she is producing is pressure!

IS YOUR PROMISE PLACING PRESSURE ON YOU?

Is your promise placing pressure on you? Pressure to perform, pressure for validation, success, productivity? Is it to the point it threatens to define your self-worth? Isn't this how we sometimes feel when we fixate on the promise? Do we feel as though we are not producing a thing? The feelings it fosters can prove almost unbearable. You may feel like giving up and the pressure of the promise hangs over your head and in your face until you are sick with it. We feel as though we may die if something doesn't happen soon. After all, why live when there is nothing to live for? It seems the very reason you are here on earth has fallen flat! Zero productivity and now nothing but this tremendous pressure! All the while, the terrible, ugly, unwanted situations you never asked for flourish!

I can imagine how friends and family must have treated Rachel. *Are you pregnant yet? When are you two going to have a baby? Isn't it about time the two of you had a child or two?* That is exactly how people treat us when they have been privy to the promise God has given us. Even if we do not expect immediate results, those around us sometimes do!

So what happens when, three years later, five years later, ten years later that Word, that promise has not yet borne fruit? The pressure is on and people are asking questions. *Didn't God give you a word about. . .? Weren't you supposed to move ahead in . . . ? Why haven't you done thus and so?* Ugh!

The lack of movement, the lack of productivity, the burden, the anxiety! It's almost more than you can take! After all, it is not like you haven't tried to bring this about. It is not like you are sitting on your hands with no clue what needs to happen here. You see it, you know the responsibility of it, you feel the weight of it, yet you, yourself, are powerless to make anything happen. Meanwhile, the promise itself keeps screaming at you to do *something, anything!*

Oh, to simply forget it all and be satisfied with the way things are. The only thing that seems to be growing and producing is everything you *never* wanted. Maybe it is time just to be satisfied with the job you have, the family you have, the church or ministry you have. So, why is it when you try to resign yourself to what is being all there is, do you experience such unrest?

Jacob wanted Rachel and now he had Rachel. He loved her. He was with her. She was in his house. Maybe that was enough? Until now, it had seemed to suffice but now she is getting cranky. There is such pressure and unrest now. Jacob only thought he had experienced tension. Jacob was not God. He was completely unable to cause Rachel to conceive. Leah had borne several children and seemingly effortlessly. *What did Rachel expect him to do?*

WHERE IS LEAH IN THE TIME OF PRESSURE?

Poor Leah! She was so unattractive and unwanted. She had endured the rejection of a husband she desired only to please. Yet he refused to embrace her and it seemed their children were of little significance to him. She must have thought how happy they might have been together if not for her high-maintenance, demanding, sister. Jacob and Leah could have learned so much from each other.

Leah is not only living with a husband who is only content with her as a baby factory but there is bad blood between her and her sister. It must have been difficult to sit back and look at her beautiful sister. Leah did everything right and everything possible to woo and win Jacob's attention and affection. Having children gave her credibility from a cultural standpoint but it seemed to pale in comparison to Rachel's beauty in her standing with Jacob.

Besides! Look what having children did to her body! She was already a bit homely and now childbirth has taken its toll. It is true, children, though a blessing, can take a toll on a body, especially when arriving one right after the other. Rachel? Well, as beautiful as ever. Too bad Jacob was so short-sighted. Leah may have been ugly but she was hands down more productive. If only Jacob had looked past the ugly and embraced her productivity.

How often do we place our focus in the wrong direction and on the wrong thing? Our attention, hopes and dreams are placed on the promise. What we want to see is the beautiful outcome of what God said to us not what difficult things it may take to prepare us for what He has promised.

We, like Jacob are stubborn, short-sighted and self-centered. We want the beauty and ease of what God has to offer but often choose not to focus on the process that brings us to that place. It is inappropriate to focus on one specific prophetic word or spoken blessing as the whole of it. God's plan is not complete in that word alone. Too much focus on the promise and ignorance of the process will bring pressure and trouble. We must realize, we must embrace the process in order to reach the beautiful pinnacle of promise.

DO YOU EMBRACE YOUR PROCESS?

An introspective look reveals much. Are you experiencing massive advancement in the ugly process with little or no progress at all in your promise? Are you praising God regardless? Have you hit a place where there is no movement at all? Do you embrace the process and what it produces as a direct route to productivity in the promise of God or are you like Jacob? Are you refusing to embrace this process no matter how productive it is because of its absolute ugliness?

As Leah named her first three children, she was constantly attempting to get Jacob to embrace, accept and love her. Leah wanted Jacob to know that beautiful or not, she was a good thing in his life. *I am good for you, I will be good for you and I can help you Jacob. If only you will give me a chance.*

The names of Leah's children reflected her mental and emotional journey through her marriage and silent competition with her sister as well as her spiritual condition. Jacob's response or lack of response to Leah and her children reflected his spiritual condition as well. He was unwilling or at best unable to embrace the ugly woman and the children she bore no matter how hard she tried or what purpose she served according to God's plan for his life.

We are no different. Like Jacob, we do everything within our power to distance ourselves from what is difficult, what we do not want or didn't ask for. The ugly, unwanted, undesirable process is forever drawing us. Still, we do our best to ignore it. If only we could realize, it would be to our benefit to embrace every detail of it wholeheartedly from the onset.

If we embrace, we find grace. If we embrace and find grace in our process our promise comes to fruition more expediently. All too often, we find ourselves needing to be processed and reprocessed before we finally accept God's way of doing things! If only we understood; the lengthy, ugly process God uses to shape and mold us is infinitely beneficial. It is imperative we remember; the process and the promise work in tandem.

COULD JACOB NOT SEE HOW GOD WAS IN CONTROL?

Was it really impossible for Jacob to see what God was doing in this situation? Did he really know God wanted Leah for him even though HE wanted Rachel? Was he still blinded by love? Really?

Sometimes we see something beautiful and assume it is *the* thing GOD wants for us. If it looks good, smells good, tastes good, then it must *be* good. God wants us to have good things, right?

But aren't we forgetting something? Romans 8:28 says God causes *all* things to work for *good*. It does not say God causes all good things to work! To God, all that he orchestrates is used for good, whether process or promise, ugly or beautiful. Ultimately, the process and everything it produces is every bit as beautiful, good and necessary as anything the promise has to offer.

SO WHAT HAPPENS NOW? – WHEN NO ONE IS PRODUCING

After Judah, Leah seemed to pull her fleshly thoughts and energy out of the race. She was content to praise God for all he had given her rather than focus on what she did not have. This is exactly what he wants from us! Give up the striving! Stop competing! Focus on developing your gifts, hearing God, interceding and nurturing the anointing and by all means, Praise the Lord in this place!

Oh, that it were that simple! If that could be the end of it; we just praise God and trouble ceases. Unfortunately, that is not exactly what happened in Leah, Rachel and Jacob's case. Leah, the ugly, unwanted, woman of process whose only redeeming quality was her ability to give Jacob children, stopped bearing for a season now they were left facing each other. Oh the tension! Oh, the desperation in the air!

So, what do you do when *nothing* is happening? Neither woman was having children. Leah had four beautiful sons. Rachel had yet to produce the first child. Then Leah has suddenly stopped bearing as well. Leah finally reaches a place she is able to simply praise God without the love of her husband and now her productivity ceases as well!

Typically, that awkward time of silence in process and promise is when people begin to move in the flesh. For us, this is usually the point we begin to in our own strength to *make* something happen. There is so much potential and yet so much pressure! We can barely stand it because absolutely nothing is producing or progressing! This can be a true trying of our faith.

NO PRODUCTION-TRIES OUR FAITH LIKE GOLD

1 Peter 1:7 speaks of the trying of our faith being more precious than perishable gold, and though it is tried with fire it might be found unto praise honor and glory at the appearing of Jesus Christ.

We often hear sermons about the goldsmith who brings the precious gold to a certain degree in the fire in order to skim the dross from it and purify the gold. After a lengthy, heated and trying process, the gold is pure and perfected. How does the goldsmith know the gold is perfected? He can see his reflection in it. God tries our faith by fire and this trying of our faith, the Bible says, is much more precious than that of gold. Why? *It does not perish.*

Sometimes we overlook the previous verse. 1 Peter 1:6 which says, *wherein ye greatly rejoice now for a season if need be, ye are in heaviness through manifold temptations* .Greatly rejoice about *what?* Greatly rejoice in that God knows exactly how much processing we can endure before we are finished. The good thing about a great and loving God is that He is willing to do whatever it requires to stretch us and purify us for His work. He knows that when purified, one ounce of pure gold can be spun out for miles. Our trying, trials, temptations and purifications enable us to be stretched as well. Purified and stretched by way of the process is what it takes to move us into the promise.

⟆⟆⟆⟆

Ishmael may have been Abraham's first born but Isaac was the promise. Jacob's brother may have appeared bigger and stronger but Jacob was the one God chose. Rachel may have been more beautiful and desirable in Jacob's eyes but ugly Leah is the one God chose for Jacob and that is *all* the validation that was needed.

Sadly, the competition was still on as far as Rachel was concerned. Now that Leah stopped bearing, Rachel had some time to play catch up. In effort to make something happen, to have a child for her beloved Jacob, Rachel decided it was time to tag out and put in a fresh face.

CHAPTER 8

Children Under Pressure - Making Something Happen

RACHEL GAVE HER MAID BILHAH (OLD OR CONFUSED)

RACHEL IS UNDER an extreme amount of pressure and she is looking for vindication wherever she can find it. Leah has a house full of babies and is hated by her husband but definitely ahead in the race if there was one. For Rachel, something must happen soon to improve her position in this family. She knows Jacob loves her but how long before his bond with these four sons of Leah begins to pull his attention away from her.

GEN 30:3 And she said, Behold (consider, take a look at) my maid Bilhah (means old or confused), go in unto her; and she shall bear upon my knees, that I may also have children by her.

Jacob, honey you know how much I want to have a baby. You know how important it is to me to give you children. Have you considered Bilhah? Rachel, introduces the idea of her concubine having children in her stead. An acceptable practice? Yes. The best idea? No. But Rachel's desperation to compete with her sister in childbearing has over ruled her common sense. Rachel though, is not about to place herself in an inferior position to Leah or anyone else, so she considers her options. She has her handmaid Bilhah whose name means one who is old or confused. The mere meaning of her name is enough to tell us Rachel was free to move ahead with her plans without threat of losing ground with her beloved Jacob. Old and confused Bilhah would simply serve a need and then be set aside.

Whether she was old or confused or both, Jacob seemed to be getting the raw end of the deal. Instead of producing a child with his beautiful, beloved Rachel, he was repeating history and going in to a handmaid, a surrogate of sorts as his grandfather had done. Not only that, her name indicates she wasn't exactly a prize winning beauty. Whether this mattered to Rachel or helped her to make this choice we do not know. Rachel simply wanted a child and only Rachel could have convinced Jacob to be a part of such a scheme.

Bilhah would bear on Rachel's knees and the child would legally be the child of Rachel and Jacob. This would place Rachel in the running with Leah. Was this the most ideal situation? No, but it was a viable option. It was an acceptable, even practical method and a means to a much desired end for Rachel.

We must be wise and sensible regarding options and choices along the path that leads to our destiny. Simply because something is an acceptable option, does not validate it as God's best for us. When we choose the alternate plan, the practical way, the acceptable practice, it is generally born out of fleshly frustration and an attempt to make our desire happen. It can complicate matters to say the least and sometimes unleash serious consequence.

BILHAH HAS DAN – JUDGMENT/VINDICATION

Gen 30:4 and she gave him Bilhah her handmaid to wife; and Jacob went in unto her. 5 And Bilhah conceived, and bare Jacob a son 6

And Rachel said, God hath judged me, and hath also heard my voice, and hath given me a son; therefore called she his name Dan.

Jacob lay with old, confused Bilhah and she brought forth the son Rachel would call Dan. Dan's name means to judge or vindication. Rachel has determined God has heard her, judged her and promptly vindicated her by giving her a son for Jacob. Though Rachel may feel fully vindicated, it is easy for us to see flesh in the works. Rachel did not trust, seek and rely on God. She decided to help God help her produce a child.

Jacob, with the more spiritual perspective and the knowledge of his grandparent's messy family situation, surely wondered whether this was the right thing to do. He knew of Hagar the slave girl and Ishmael her son but if he ever thought it to be a risky plan, it is not recorded.

Are we looking for God to vindicate us or judge our situation? Many times, we are. The trouble is, judgment *does* come when we step out into the arena of the flesh and attempt to MAKE things happen but vindication, not necessarily. When we tamper with God's plan, judgment is often necessary but we err to think it comes in the form of vindication, validation or exoneration.

BILHAH HAS NAPHTALI - STRUGGLE

Apparently the short-lived vindication Rachel felt was not enough. Eventually her desire to have another child through her handmaid surfaced. The struggle with her sister Leah was intense and it must have been difficult for Rachel to watch as Jacob's sons ran to their father jumping into his arms and sitting at his feet as he rested at the end of the day. Rachel desperately wanted children.

Still showing no signs of conceiving, she found it easier to convince Jacob to employ the services of Bilhah once again. At the news of Bilhah's conception Rachel felt as though she had prevailed in her competition with her older sister Leah. The name of the child was Naphtali, meaning *my struggle.*

Gen. 30:7 And Bilhah Rachel's maid conceived again and bare Jacob a second son. 8 And Rachel said, with great wrestlings have I wrestled with my sister and I have prevailed, and she called his name Naphtali.

Take note of Jacob's actions. Rather than refuse, he indulged Rachel's whim to have yet another child through her handmaid. Rather than turn and embrace Leah, who may have been ugly but was the God chosen vessel to complete a process within Jacob. He chose to go in yet again to handmaid whose name alone tells you she was in no better condition than poor ugly Leah.

Not just once but *twice* he bore children with this woman to please the beautiful wife he loved so. Yet what did this union produce? It only produced more struggle. Rachel's search for further justice and vindication only produced further struggle and complication, still not solving the problem of barrenness.

It seemed Rachel had prospered in her fleshly act of giving her husband her handmaid and with no apparent repercussions of that initial act. It seemed a good idea to repeat the process. After all, it had become more about head counting and competition with Leah than anything else. Rachel assumed herself winning!

Examine Rachel's motive. It seems she was not nearly as interested in giving her husband a family as she was in getting on over on her ugly sister Leah! Rachel says, *I have wrestled with my sister and I have prevailed.* The struggle was not as much in her inability to give her husband what he desired but between the two girls. Rachel feels she has gained the upper hand.

This also reveals how far Jacob will go to please Rachel. Is it possible at this juncture, his actions are more a maneuver to get her off his back? By giving in to Rachel's handmaid sharing, Jacob was inadvertently placing his covenant covered future in jeopardy, just as Abraham did with Ishmael. By this time beautiful Rachel threatened to become an idol opening the door to the flesh which could ultimately cost Jacob everything.

When we choose a fleshly remedy like Jacob and Rachel, we invite judgment upon ourselves. This is a prime example of how far *we* will go to avoid the process. We will go out of the way to avoid the correct choice because another way seems easier or more acceptable rather than simply *do* what is right and follow through. The struggle it creates is in no way beneficial.

The struggle between Rachel and Leah has become a full blown war with another innocent child named Naphtali at the center and Rachel feeling rather superior at the moment. Not only can she claim two sons as hers now, she has the satisfaction of knowing she remains her husband's favorite. Rachel is quite confident still that she is the keeper of Jacob's heart.

We, like Rachel, have a tendency to allow a struggle to ensue when we do not feel our destiny is unfolding as it should. This should not be. The process and the promise are designed to work together.

When we allow pride, envy and struggle to work its way in, we are not pliable as God desires. The struggle to stay on top causes us to remain competitive and aggressive. We tend to adopt an *"it's all about me and I'll show them what I can do"* attitude that is completely out of line with God's will and plan.

Why was Rachel jealous of Leah? Why such struggle between the two? It makes no sense. Rachel was obviously more beautiful, younger and favored by their husband Jacob. It seems Rachel would have been quite secure. She had a grace that Leah did not. Could it be Rachel recognized something that neither Jacob nor Leah realized? That sweet young thing of beauty may have realized how much less weight her looks would carry in the end. Beauty is fleeting.

It is important not to place too much importance on the actual promise, word spoken, Minister delivering the word or the sketched picture of the end result. Though we delight in the beautiful picture before us, there is an ugly process we must first embrace. We cannot rely too heavily on the beauty and completely disregard the difficulties, the struggle, the process we must endure in order to bring us to the place God promised. We misunderstand, we misconstrue.

Though it may not be as beautiful, graceful and glamorous the fruit bearing process desires our embrace in the way that Leah desired Jacob's. The beautiful promise brings beauty and hope that keeps us reaching but it is obvious that the growth and maturity comes through the things produced by the ugly process. It is our Leah. It is our ugly woman. It is our ugly process that keeps producing what will become our future and producing with seemingly no effort at all!

Both the promise and the process have their place and purpose in our lives. There should be no envy or jockeying for position between the two. Without both, prosperity cannot come. Without both, fulfillment is impossible. Yet we lean toward what is more appealing to our senses. We believe if it is more beautiful, it is right. Not so. Rarely is that so.

Competition cultivated by Rachel's inability to bare children seemed to spur each of them on. It seemed to highlight beautiful Rachel's insecurity while vindicating the ugly woman Leah.

Leah was not pretty but there was a depth in her that Rachel never attained. She had a strength Rachel did not possess. Leah stepped back and sought God for answers, attempting to please Jacob and building her family in an unassuming fashion. Brick by brick she built a house with this man. She was solid, stable, and gracious in spite of all that was against her.

Rachel's subconscious understanding of Leah's importance in the life of her beloved felt threatening to her. Rachel was all about Rachel.

Beautiful, yet contained and confined to a certain level of productivity. When the pressure was on, Rachel behaved in an ugly, competitive way, while the difficulty of Leah's circumstance made her more productive. Leah was becoming somewhat more attractive.

ZILPAH HAS GAD – A TROOP - PROCESS STILL PRODUCING

Gen 30:9-11 NIV When Leah saw that she had stopped having children, she took her maidservant Zilpah and gave her to Jacob as a wife. Leah's servant Zilpah bore Jacob a son. The Leah said, "What good fortune!" So she named him Gad.

Leah meanwhile, was watching Rachel build her little family. Even though she had more children, she knew she was not loved by Jacob. When Leah saw she had left bearing and Rachel had found a way to produce children for Jacob, she decided to get in on the action. True, Leah had reached a place of praising God anyway when the production of such a fine group of sons was not enough to make Jacob fall in love with her. Still, she decided she should further secure her position.

Surely they were enough to keep the upper hand or maybe for just a moment, doubt ensued. Right now, it seemed Jacob's attention is pulled back toward Rachel and her drama. Rachel's policy of producing children through her maid apparently inspired Leah to do likewise and by this method, Jacob could have more sons. After all, it was acceptable and apparently accepted by Jacob.

Though she should have refrained from delving into the flesh as Rachel had, Leah too gave Jacob her handmaid. Zilpah, whose name means a cleansing or refinement, bare Jacob a son Leah would name Gad. Gad means good fortune or a troop cometh. Leah must have thought to herself; *Ahhh, I may be ugly but I can certainly produce those sons!*

Leah may not have given birth to this son but it was a son. Whether by her or her handmaid, in Jacob's family a troop was coming. Leah may be down but she was not out. She would continue to produce for this man and maybe, just maybe he would someday realize her value.

Has a lull in productivity of process or promise caused you to feel outnumbered or a bit nervous that the odds may be stacked against you? Watching others flourish in ministry can be daunting when nothing is happening in yours but you must press on. We must continue, no matter what it looks like, no matter how bleak it looks, God is in control of what is and what is *not* happening. His hand is on us and angels are all about ministering to and for us.

God has allowed the trampling we feel but only for our testing. He is assessing what we are made of and showing us all we can accomplish through Him. In the process we may feel a bit out of sorts as it seems we fail and our rivals prevail but if we follow through with His process, we triumph in the end.

ZILPAH HAS ASHER – HAPPINESS – PROCESS WILL ULTIMATELY BRING HAPPINESS

Gen 30:12-13 NIV Leah's servant Zilpah bore Jacob a second son. Then Leah said, "How happy I am! The women will call me happy." So she named him Asher.

Having experienced such good fortune with the birth of Gad, again Leah chose Zilpah to give birth in her stead. It was a son, Jacob's eighth son, Leah's sixth and she named him Asher which means happiness. Yet another son continued to confirm God's presence in the marriage of Jacob to this ugly, unwanted woman.

Leah had found a place of praise when she had Judah even though she had not won the desired affection of Jacob. After she saw Rachel giving her handmaid to bear her children, Leah also chose that route. By this time, Leah knew she had God's favor but it must have been a little unnerving to see Jacob and Rachel share the bond of a child. It is not surprising that this bit of insecurity would come about even after she had developed such security.

Even after praise has developed through our process there can be other issues needing exposed. When we think we have finally conquered our fears and erased our insecurities, the enemy will come in on the sly.

It almost seemed there was a sense of relief as Zilpah bore these two sons and confirmed yet again, her significance in Jacob's life. Though it seemed she should be reassured, it simply shows that even after we reach a place of praise we sometimes need reminded and reinforced in our thinking.

Rachel took matters into her own hands with respect to her handmaid and though it appeared she moved forward. In reality, she lost ground. Leah too was inspired to give her handmaid and though this was not necessary since she had these other sons, the Lord blessed her with two more sons. Confirming to us that the promise will not supersede the process God initiates.

CHAPTER **9**

How About Those Apples?

JACOB HIRED WITH MANDRAKES

RACHEL MUST HAVE taken pause as Leah's maid Zilpah bore Jacob two sons in Leah's stead. Leah didn't need to give Zilpah to Jacob. Rachel's ugly sister had borne Jacob half a dozen male children for Jacob. No matter, Rachel still had security knowing she was Jacob's favorite. She would simply wait for yet another opportunity. It would not be long before opportunity presented itself.

Genesis 30:14 NIV During wheat harvest, Reuben went out into the fields and found some mandrake plants, which he brought to his mother Leah. Rachel said to Leah, "Please give me some of your son's mandrakes."

It is quite obvious at this time that Jacob's family is growing. Reuben, Jacob's first son, old enough to be in the field during wheat harvest, found mandrakes. Those knowing what mandrakes are immediately understand why the possession of this plant, its root or its fruit would be important to someone like Rachel.

Mandrake in Hebrew means love plant. The root of the mandrake can be shaped like male or female bodies. It was powerful enough to be used as an anesthesia and said to shriek when pulled up by the root. The superstition was that getting your hands on this plant or its fruit was tedious because it would kill the one pulling it up from the ground.

The important characteristic for Rachel was that it was thought to be an aphrodisiac that would help barren women produce children. If too much of the plant was given to a man, he might be knocked out or even killed. If the proper amount was given, children were the result.

The power it was thought to hold was well known enough that Reuben brought it straight home to his mother and word quickly spread that Leah had acquired mandrakes. Something else notable is that this also tells us that Leah's lack of favor as the wife of Jacob was widely known as well.

Word was out. This was big news and Rachel, thinking of Rachel of course, was willing to grovel for the mandrakes if that is what it took to obtain the superstitious root/fruit. Rachel said, *Give me, I pray thee, of thy son's mandrakes.* This could be just the thing she needed to relieve her anguish and bring forth a child of her own. Leah was appalled at Rachel's audacity.

Gen. 30:15 NIV But she said to her, "Wasn't it enough that you took away my husband? Will you take my son's mandrakes too?"

It seems the feud between the sisters would never end. Leah said, *Is it a small matter that you have taken my husband? Now, you want my sons mandrakes also?* Rachel's request for the mandrakes seemed to disgust Leah. *You, Rachel, the woman who has the heart and favor of the husband who is rightfully mine and you have the nerve to ask for something else that is not rightfully yours? How like you Rachel. How typical of you to think about yourself before others.*

Rachel was not deterred by any feelings of repugnance Leah felt. She simply chose a different strategy. She knew what Leah would want and she was ready to make a deal. Rachel wanted those mandrakes. She decided to make Leah and offer she could not refuse. *Give me the mandrakes and Jacob will lie with you tonight.*

Was this plant really worth that much to Rachel? Obviously, it was. Rachel needed a baby from her own body. The mandrakes were exactly what she needed to seal the deal. She knew she was loved. The only thing she lacked was to give her beloved Jacob children and she felt certain the mandrakes would make that possible.

Rachel nonchalantly offers up her beloved husband to Leah for one night. It seems odd she would readily offer him when she had seen how Leah produced children early on. Her trading of Jacob for the night showed one thing clearly; she was not at all nervous that her adoring husband would be lost to her after time spent with her older, uglier sister. What made her so sure of herself? Was it her vanity regarding her beauty? Was it Jacob's treatment of her or maybe his mistreatment of Leah? Did she place such value and confidence in the mandrakes that she thought his night with ugly Leah was more than worth the trade?

Why did Leah not keep the mandrakes for herself? She obviously trusted God and did not believe in the superstitious power of the plant as Rachel did. As far as she was concerned, the mandrakes held no real value to her in her relationship with Jacob. She had children and she simply was not one to place much value on idolatry or superstition. Leah's interest was not in the mandrakes or what it could do for her but in how the possession of it could be bartered to give her precious time with Jacob.

Was it her spiritual standing? Did she realize that even though Jacob outwardly rejected her, God was on her side? She had earlier credited God with her blessed womb, therefore she was likely much more spiritually wise than her younger sister. She did not rely on anyone other than God to provide what she needed. Rachel had dabbled in idolatry and witchcraft before and this was nothing other than more of the same. Leah was not so easily fooled. She knew she did not need mandrakes to produce. She already had a fruitful womb but in order to produce another beautiful child she did need one very important thing—JACOB! For this reason, the deal was worth making.

ᴐᴐᴐ

Leah did not bother to meet Jacob at the door. The trust between her and her sister was at an all-time low. She knew that if Jacob came in from the field it would not be her door. Everyone knew he would set out for Rachel's tent and would take the scenic route in order to avoid passing Leah on the way. If this happened, Leah would stand no chance of spending one minute, much less the whole night with Jacob. She dare not trust Rachel to keep her end of the bargain. Leah's answer to this dilemma was to meet him as he came in from the field. If Leah's eyesight was as bad as some believe, this was no easy feat. Jacob could be any number of places and she must find him before he reached Rachel's tent. What determination, fortitude and resolve Leah had.

Listen Jacob, you MUST come in unto me; for I have hired you with my son's mandrakes. Maybe you do not really want to but I have bought you for a price. Tonight, you belong to me. And he lay with her that night. What was Leah feeling that night? Had she gone to great lengths to make it as special as possible or was the whole night plagued with the realization that Rachel had mandrakes and tomorrow, Jacob would be with her again. Maybe Leah used that fact to entice Jacob. I've given Rachel my mandrakes. If you lie with me tonight, tomorrow, your chances for a son with her are greater. Either way, her wisdom in not trusting in the potential and idolatry of the mandrakes was rewarded by God when she conceived Issachar, their fifth son.

LEAH HAS ISSACHAR- REWARD/RECOMPENSE/REIMBURSEMENT

Gen 30:17 NIV God listened to Leah, and she became pregnant and bore Jacob a fifth son. Then Leah said, "God has rewarded me for giving my maidservant to my husband." So she named him Issachar.

It had been some time since Leah had had a child and both women had provided a total of four sons for Jacob through their handmaids in the interim. The child that came through the giving up of the mandrakes to Rachel was Issachar, whose name means reward or recompense. God was rewarding Leah and Jacob with yet another son.

Throughout the Bible we see bounty given for battle and in this way Leah enjoyed bounty for the battle she lived on a daily basis. Every day she watched her beautiful sister and her husband so in love while she was the one bearing fruit. She is the one suffering and giving Jacob what is important; the children who would become the innumerable seed the blessing had promised. Beautiful Rachel is looking beautiful but has not been able to offer much else other than nagging and manipulation.

Leah made what might have seemed like a foolish choice when she gave away the mandrakes or love. It may have seemed the right choice to keep them for herself and hope that Jacob would eventually come in to her, but that is not what she did. She chose to allow God to handle her fertility and strike the deal simply to get Jacob into her tent. Her wisdom was rewarded and she was paid back for the trouble she suffered with yet another son.

Leah reasoned that God had rewarded her for giving her maid to Jacob and repaid her for having lost his affection to Rachel. Who knows, Jacob may have grown to love Leah if Rachel had not been part of the deal. Still, God had been faithful to her and blessed her with an open womb and sons.

God saw Leah's heart and when He did, He gave her Issachar. He gave her a reward, recompense, a reimbursement for her troubles, repayment for the love she had missed. Who knows, maybe there was some evidence of relationship growing with Jacob by this time. Leah had faithfully called out to God and God was now rewarding her for that attitude and faithfulness. Likewise, as we seek God through and embrace our process, reward and recompense come to us. The Word of God reminds us in Hebrews 11:6 that God is a rewarder of those who diligently seek Him.

LEAH HAS ZEBULUN – DWELLING/CONTENTMENT

Gen 30:19 And Leah conceived again, and bare Jacob the sixth son. 20 And Leah said, God hath endued me with a good dowry; now will my husband dwell with me, because I have born him six sons; and she called his name Zebulun.

Genesis 30:19 NIV says, *And Leah conceived again. . .*

Could it be that Jacob and Leah have finally found a place of coexistence? Apparently Jacob visited Leah again at some point after Issachar's birth because she conceived again. Another son!

Had Jacob begun to see ugly Leah for the beauty she really was? Leah longed for love from Jacob but she had come to a place of contentment. Maybe Jacob did not love her like he loved Rachel but acknowledge her, he must. This ugly woman Jacob was forced to live with played a significant role. By now, there was no denying it.

Leah had reached a place of certainty that she would prevail. She said, *God hath endued me with a good dowry, now will my husband dwell with me, because I have born him six sons. Jacob will finally be pleased and content to have me.*

The Bible tells us in Proverbs 16:8 NIV that *better is a little with righteousness than great revenues without right.* Leah may not have everything exactly as she hoped but she had finally come to realize, she had enough. Leah realized God was on her side. She had cried unto Him and He had heard her cry every time.

We never find Leah saying, *Oh well, I didn't really want that anyway.* She wanted Jacob to love her but she had come to a place of acceptance where that was not the important thing. Her contentment with God was all that really mattered.

Philippians 4:12 NIV says, *I know what it is to be in need, and I know what it is to have plenty. I have learned the secret of being content in any and every situation.* This scripture came well after Leah's time but at this point in her life it was undoubtedly her sentiment.

She was blessed, she was hated and she had given birth to six sons of her own and two by her handmaid by now. Leah had learned to dwell in a state of contentment. We have to wonder what state Jacob was in when Zebulun was born. Where did Jacob *dwell*? Did he dwell in contentment as Leah? It looked as though maybe Jacob was at least finding a place of acceptance of his circumstances.

Jacob was blessed with children as God had promised. True, Jacob's desire was that these sons might all have come through beautiful Rachel but this was not the case. Whether willingly or by God's gentle persuasion Jacob must accept that these beautiful covenant fulfilling offspring were born of ugly Leah. It was becoming more and more impossible to discount her value.

1 Timothy 6:6 NIV tells us, *Godliness with contentment is great gain.* Contentment and Godliness go together. One does not develop without the other. Contentment comes as you work your way through your God-ordained process and the acceptance of what has been offered you.

When we focus on the promise and overlook the process we easily become discontent. Intently focusing on the promise itself is a breeding ground for discontentment coupled with a refusal to embrace the process. It is only as the process is completed in our lives that we see contentment.

Unless we weather the storms and trials God allows in our lives with patience and faith and a willingness to truly forego contention for the sake of contentment, we will never find true fulfillment. If we stop short we will experience the toil and labor of the grueling process without the full circle of the two together. When we surrender to God and His perfect will even when it does not match our imperfect desires, we will find a satisfied place to dwell.

Zebulun was the sixth son and six is the biblical number of man. During our process we have to come to the place we are content to dwell with the Lord and to dwell in His ways. He said if ye abide or dwell in me and my word abide or dwell in you then you can ask what you will and it shall be done unto you.

Leah was counting on God to come through for her concerning her husband. She had placed herself and her situation in God's hands and demonstrated a willingness to accept whatever came with a right heart and a good attitude. She was ugly and hated but knew enough to hide herself in the secret place of the most high, hiding under the shadow of God almighty. It was there that she matured and there contentment found a place to dwell.

We do well to learn from Leah's example. At this juncture, she has found a level of contentment and acceptance. It may not be a good place but is definitely a Godly place. It seems as we go through the process we gain wisdom and understanding. We are able to find a place of contentment where we are because we know this is the place God has us. If what we long for never happens, it never happens. We are at ease with the situation and what it has become. Contentment really is great gain.

Zebulun, the child of contentment for Leah, gave her hope she might gain honor with her husband. According to later blessing in his life, Zebulun would dwell by the sea as a haven for ships. As it were, even from birth, Zebulun was truly a haven, or dwelling place of contentment for Leah. When he was born, Leah finally decided to lay it all down and be satisfied or at least at ease with God and His will.

There was the gift, representing the strong hope of a future with her husband. There was the hearing and anointing. She found a place of praise that carried her through a time she bore no fruit. There was the little slip into acceptable, yet fleshly actions that still yet gave her and Jacob two other sons. Gad and Asher would yet multiply her husband's family bringing Leah happiness and a sense of satisfaction.

So much blessing, yet the love of her husband remained with her sister. Still, the life she had was much better than the one she might have had. She and her children were safe and their heritage strong. Her life and her marital situation, or lack thereof, could have proven to be much worse.

Contentment, satisfaction, agreement--all familiar words yet they seem a bit isolated and inaccessible at times. We are forever *looking* for that place of contentment, when in fact we should be content in this place. If only we could fully understand there is a haven for us, a place of protection and safety when we determine to be content with what *is* -exactly as it is.

The real lesson for us; give up the love apples! Go ahead and give up the thing that *looks* like it is going to take you to your destination. Let it go. Release it. It's over. It's gone and just when it looks as though it's gone for good reward, recompense and contentment follow! For Leah; more sons! Additions to the family of process! Pieces of the puzzle! More children from the ugly underappreciated woman to bring Jacob into the promise!

LEAH HAD DINAH-JUSTICE/VALIDITY/CONCLUSION

The Bible says that sometime later, Leah gave birth to a daughter and called her Dinah. Dinah means justice or judgment, vindication or validation. Not the fleshly validation or vindication that Rachel sought through the birth of Dan from her handmaid but justice due Leah. It was the validation she deserved as God's chosen process for maturity and growth in the life of Jacob.

Dan, meaning vindication was born out of Rachel's taking matters into her own hands. Dinah, meaning validation came through a divine process. Both mean judgment. Only one is the God given conclusion. Dinah was child number seven for Leah. The competition had been fierce. It did not matter they had gotten into the fleshly realm by presenting their maids to produce children. It did not matter whether Leah was ugly and Rachel was beautiful. It did not matter if Rachel was loved and Leah hated.

Hold steady! Leah, the ugly process has been vindicated! Leah, the ugly process has produced justice!

In our process, what others say, do or think does not matter. Our judgment, vindication and validation come from the God of process and promise! It doesn't matter how others have lied, misrepresented, misunderstood or whatever!

God will bring justice to us *just as* he did Leah. He will make it . . .

Just as if I have never been hated!

Just as if I have never been rejected!

Just as if I have never failed!

Just as if I have never backslidden!

Just as if life had never gone exactly opposite the way I desired it to go!

Just as if I have never done anything *but* please and praise the Lord!

The truth of the matter is this-*It ain't over 'til it's over!*

Dinah was the child of completion or conclusion. She signifies validity of Jacob's process. Dinah might be casually considered God's gravy for Leah in a long and trying test of endurance. She was the completion of the process. Rachel, the promise, can now begin to bear fruit. Rachel's maid had borne Jacob two sons but Rachel bore no children until Leah had born him seven!

It is when the process is complete that our promise is loosed to bear fruit. Romans 2:11 says there is not respect of persons with God. When the process is complete, then and *only* then will the focus of our love and attention generate fulfillment. Ugly Leah, these half dozen sons and this beautiful daughter were the ones through which Jacob would learn and experience the most. Through them he acquired the tools needed to carry out God's covenant.

Dinah means vindicated, suggesting Leah believed God was finally vindicating her in the struggle with Rachel over the affections of Jacob. Jacob came in to Leah at least two more times after she hired him. Possibly he had begun to come in to Leah not because he felt obligated but because he desired her. No other love apple *deals* were recorded and as to whether or not Rachel conceived with the help of the mandrakes, apparently *not*. I don't think so!

Maybe there had been a change in Jacob. Maybe after all this time something was drawing him to begin embracing this ugly, unwanted woman and her children. Sharing children with someone is powerful. If he still had no real love for Leah, Jacob must surely have come to respect and cherish her for strength of character she demonstrated and the beautiful offspring she gave him. As he gazed at each one, he may have noticed Leah's smile, heard her voice or seen her courage and fortitude. Could it be that Leah wasn't so ugly after all;

especially when you compare her to the barren, unproductive, high maintenance, pressing promise?

Sure, Rachel was beautiful to look at, to think about, to be with but extremely high maintenance and difficult to keep happy. Leah was not. Rachel was the apple of Jacob's eye but the constant nagging about the lack of children was maddening. Could this combination of circumstances have helped to drive him *away* from the beautiful promise Rachel and *toward* the ugly process Leah? Zebulun's name, *a place or dwelling of contentment* seems to suggest this possibility. Dinah's name, *justice*, appears to solidify the thought.

CHAPTER 10

Over-Processed - As Gorgeous As It Gets

LEAH BORE JACOB SEVEN CHILDREN
BEFORE RACHEL BORE HIM ONE

LEAH BORE JACOB seven children; six sons and a daughter. This is significant because the number seven is the number of completion. Leah continued to bear Jacob's children until there were seven. She produced until there was a completion of the process. Seven children for this man of promise and her task was complete.

Rachel though, had yet to give birth to one child for her darling Jacob. What Jacob thought would make his life complete remained barren and unproductive. The hope Jacob held for a beautiful life and a large family with Rachel alone would never be realized according to expectation. Any reality to the fantasies of sons with her eyes and his hair, her hands and his nose, seemed out of the question. Somewhere along the line, they had obviously adapted to the reality but the emotional agony of it was still painfully real.

MUST BE AWARE OF WEAKNESSES – THEIRS AND OURS

In each of Leah and Jacob's children of process we see our process as well. In the meaning of their names we find a representation of our gift, ability to hear, the priestly anointing, intercession, praise, strength, happiness, reward, recompense and the vindication of God. As much as the literal children were given as a part of Jacob's process and a part of the blessing of the covenant upon his life, we find the very meanings of their names parallel our process as well.

Just as God did not forget what he promised Jacob, as far back as his grandfather Abraham; God has not forgotten his promise to us. He has promised increase and increase will come but our maturity, peace and fulfillment, all come through the process.

The reward or recompense that comes when we choose to trust God is truly amazing! There is peace and contentment after we have passed tests of character and moral fiber. Only then can we see how God has brought justice and vindication to our difficult situation.

We must understand that without an intimate relationship with God, our gift, anointing or hearing cannot be trusted to act or respond properly. Without true praise, all is pointless. Progress would simply cease.

Just as each of their children eventually demonstrated weaknesses and flaws of character and integrity, Leah, Rachel and Jacob exhibit those as well. Sadly, nothing has changed. You and I exhibit the same weaknesses and flaws. Through identifying with these examples, we become more aware of our own weaknesses and realize without God's direction we are powerless and increase will never come. Without the cultivation of our gift, hearing, anointing and praise, our strength, happiness, reward, recompense and contentment will not come. Without these, we are unprepared and unworthy of the promise.

GOD REMEMBERED RACHEL-THE PROMISE PRODUCES

And God remembered. . . . It was at the point Leah stopped bearing that the Bible says, God remembered Rachel and listened to her and opened her womb. *Oh yes, Rachel, I remember. Rachel, she's the pretty one. Rachel, she's the seemingly strong one. Rachel, she's the one who captured Jacob's attention. Rachel. The importance was in the process. The numbers came from Leah, the ugly one. But yes, I remember the promise. I remember what I told you that day, in that service, in that lonely room, in that place of despair, in the time of need. I remember. I made a promise to you, a covenant with you and now, you're finally ready for it. I will bring it to pass.*

Rachel did not die from having no children as she supposed she might. You have to wonder if she ever realized she should never have spoken to Jacob the way she did about her barrenness. Did she finally realize Jacob was not responsible for her barrenness? After all, he had no problem fathering children with Leah or the handmaids of both women.

The covenant between God and Jacob was God's doing; the process by which He brought it about, His perfect plan. The trickery Jacob experienced at the hand of Laban was allowed by God to develop Jacob's character. The barrenness of Rachel until the time Leah had borne Jacob a perfect number of children was no surprise to God. The coming of a child through Rachel, the representative of the promise only after Leah, the representative of the process was finished bearing was no accident. Every detail was according to plan.

God knew Jacob had to be prepared for the promise. He had to go through some things before he was ready for Rachel's child and the events that would follow. If Rachel had borne children first, he might never have had the first child with ugly Leah. Leah's children were absolutely essential to making the covenant God had made with Jacob a reality. If Jacob had not fathered children with Leah, the majority of his family would be non-existent.

God wasn't caught off guard. God wasn't confused about the chain of events, issues at hand or the need for the promise to produce. He knew exactly how it all should go and so it went. God knew the process must come first but when it was time, God remembered Rachel. He listened to her. God opened Rachel's womb and at long last, Rachel had a child.

RACHEL HAS JOSEPH

Rachel, beautiful Rachel was finally having a baby! Can you imagine the fanfare in the family regarding the news? There was likely celebration like there had never been before!

Rachel's reaction? She said, *God has taken away my reproach! Finally, he's listening to my cries. Finally, my womb has opened up and I will name him Joseph, meaning may God increase because now that I am bearing, I know there will be more. This will not be the only one. Now that I have a breakthrough, I know there will be another son. I am no longer barren.*

Once again, though, Rachel speaks without thinking it through. In her fit of excitement at the blessed event, did she not realize her prophetic words could quite possibly place limitations on her childbearing?

We've learned already, Rachel was not known for guarding her speech. This was not the first time she would speak out of turn. She had a tendency toward and desire for more, bigger and better.

Is it possible she inadvertently cut herself short with her own words? *The Lord shall add to me another son*, she said. *I know this won't be the only one* is what she meant but who knows, maybe the Lord would have added many more sons to Rachel had she guarded her speech and simply exhibited gratefulness for the child in her arms instead of already trying to acquire more and more for the future.

We must be careful not to shortchange ourselves with our own words regarding God's promise. It is unfathomable what He might do and on what scale he might do it. When we see our promise begin to manifest and God move on our behalf, we should not think we know where or how far the fruit of the promise will reach any more than we knew when or where our promise would begin to produce. Our inability to see the big picture and the utterance of well-meant but misspoken words may inadvertently limit our productiveness.

God has so much more for us than we can imagine. It has been said before and often but bears repeating; He knows our capabilities and limitations and has orchestrated the perfect plan for our lives. If we would simply embrace it and move forward with His direction.

For Jacob, embracing God's plan has been anything but simple. Yet, God, in his faithfulness has kept His word and now Rachel has given him a son! Ohhhh, beautiful little Joseph! How Jacob must have beamed when he looked at that child! Years he had waited for his beautiful Rachel to bear him a child and now, a son, a beautiful son, named Joseph! How is it that in this stage of life something so wonderful could come to him!

Joseph's name means *may God increase* and the Bible teaches that Jacob loved Joseph more than all of his children because he was the son of his old age. Think about this; Jacob had been waiting on Joseph's arrival for a very long time. For years and years they had tried to have children. Jacob was not a young man when he met Rachel. With each passing year hope must have lessened. If you have ever struggled to have one child when people all around you are having them seemingly by the dozen, you know the joy Jacob and Rachel felt when they had Joseph.

Interestingly enough, Joseph would ultimately receive preferential treatment from his father. This special treatment was something Jacob was used to, remember? His mother had favored him above his brother Esau and his father Isaac had favored Esau. If you are familiar with Joseph's story you know that this was a common practice in Jacob's life that would prove to make Joseph's life very difficult but would without a doubt become a portion of Joseph's process and promise as well.

The upside for Joseph? He would ultimately embrace the process God used to prepare him for his promise and thereby save Egypt from famine and preserve the nation of Israel.

AFTER JOSEPH WAS BORN – JACOB DECIDES TO GO HOME - JACOB'S HEART PREPARES FOR RECONCILIATION

Gen 30:25 NIV After Rachel gave birth to Joseph, Jacob said to Laban, Send me on my way so I can go back to my own homeland.

After Rachel had Joseph, it occurred to Jacob that it was time to go to his own place and his own country. *Laban, you know how I have served you. Now give me my wives and children that I have served you for and let me go my own way.*

Did you notice Jacob said *wives?* He not only wanted to take Rachel, his beautiful promise and their precious son, Joseph, the increase of promise but he wanted to take Leah, the ugly woman of process and all her offspring. Jacob was ready to return and face his past. He wanted to go home. Yet, once more Laban would talk him into staying and naming his wage.

Jacob had been cheated so many times by Laban. He decided this time, no, no wages, just let me pick certain of the flock as my wages. That way, my righteousness will answer for me in time to come. You will know that every one of them in my possession and not per our agreement will be considered stolen by me. It seemed a good idea to Laban. After all, there was no downside for him.

Actually, it went well for both men but Jacob had been feeding these flocks a long time. It seems he had learned a thing or two about their mating habits and began to place them in such a way that the stronger would mate with each other. With this system in place and keeping his flock separate, Jacob became exceedingly prosperous.

JACOB IS BLESSED BUT LABAN'S SONS ACCUSE HIM - LABAN'S COUNTENANCE CHANGES TOWARD HIM

In light of Jacob's prosperity, Laban's sons begin to accuse Jacob of taking what was Laban's and apparently convinced Laban of the same. His countenance changed toward Jacob and Jacob saw it was no longer favorable toward him. It was time for a change of scenery.

Jacob called his wives to him in the field and told them that God was at the helm of all that was happening. God had blessed him. He was not cheating Laban. God visited Jacob in a dream. Sharing all that God had told him from the first visit until now, he told Leah and Rachel; God says, it's time to go.

JACOB'S EYES WERE OPENED TO LABAN

Every time Laban changed Jacob's wages it was due to selfish motive. He intended to cheat Jacob or keep him in a subservient position. Laban saw God's favor on Jacob. He knew this was a covenant man. It was malicious and selfish on Laban's part but all part of Jacob's process. Nothing escaped God's attention.

Jacob had always looked for his help to come from someone. Jacob had no ambition in the beginning. His mother wanted him to have the blessing of his father and he went along with it. It seemed easy enough and Jacob always desired things that came easy. Is it not sad that everything from that point on seemed to come to him at such a difficult and high price? He spent many years working diligently for his self-serving father-in-law.

Laban was the first one Jacob had dealt with uprightly. He likely believed Laban would do the same. Not so. True, Laban had taken Jacob in when he had no place to go but now he was taking advantage of him. Jacob had to come to the realization Laban could do nothing for him. He had to recognize it was God who made the promise.

Jacob came to a place during the process that he realized Laban was using him. Of course Laban wanted him to stay. Finally, Jacob's eyes were opened and he stood up to Laban. *No. There is nothing you have that I need. There is nothing here for me.*

As long as we look to others for help and not to God, we stand to be taken advantage of. Others will take advantage if we elevate them to a position belonging to God.

᳕᳕᳕

Finally Rachel and Leah were in agreement about at least one thing; their father. He had devoured all of their inheritance and sold them to Jacob for seven years of work each. Both women agreed that there was nothing left for them in their father's house. He had basically sold them both and consumed what might have been their portions. *So, really Jacob, all that belongs to you is that which belonged to us.* They believed God had blessed Jacob with all that was theirs anyway. They both agreed to follow him. So they did. *You do what God has told you and we are with you.*

Rachel got one last dig at her father by stealing his idols. Why? It was doubtful she stole them for monetary value. Possibly she believed in whatever fortune they might bring. When looking back, she was the one who traded her husband to her sister for a night for the supposedly charmed root/fruit of the mandrake. She had previously demonstrated she was the one prone to idolatry and superstition.

JACOB FLEES

Jacob once again found himself looking over his shoulder as he fled. This is reminiscent of when he left home. He was not necessarily under the threat of death but had certainly left without facing Laban.

Laban was quite territorial. Though he had given his daughters and maids to Jacob, he still considered them his property along with the children produced from both marriages. Having been privy to details of Jacob's initial flight from home, Laban felt secure. He had no thought Jacob would ever return home and risk being killed by his brother Esau. Jacob's presence in Laban's life had actually increased Laban greatly. Still, Laban likely preferred to think he had done Jacob the favor by allowing him to serve him all these years.

Have you had the experience of working alongside someone like Laban? The blessing of God falls on your endeavors only to have them feel as though *they* have somehow done you a favor? God's children are blessed. The anointing and the favor of the Lord on them often inadvertently blesses those whose lives they touch. Sadly, those not surrendered to the Lord may feel as though *they* are responsible for or even entitled to the good that has come to you and yours.

GOD WARNS LABAN NOT TO SPEAK GOOD OR BAD TO JACOB

Any thought Jacob may have had regarding Laban's feelings about his departure would prove to be more than accurate. Laban *was* very angry. He was angry enough to pursue Jacob personally for seven days before overtaking him in the mount of Gilead.

What exactly did he plan to do when he caught up with Jacob? We don't really know but he went after him nonetheless. God knew Laban's intentions though because he came to Laban in a dream and warned him not to say anything to Jacob, good or bad. The Bible warns to use care in what you say to God's anointed and Laban knew enough to heed God's warning.

Laban certainly had some questions for Jacob. *What have you done that you had to run? Did you take my daughters captive with a sword? I might have sent you away with a party but you didn't even allow me to kiss my children. How foolish that was Jacob! I have the power to hurt you but the God of your father spoke to me last night and warned me not to speak to you good or bad. Obviously, you have gone because you are very homesick but why did you steal my gods?*

Jacob explained to Laban his reason for leaving. He left the way he did out of fear Laban would take his daughters away by force. Still, Jacob knew nothing of the stolen gods. *With whomever you find your gods, do not let him live!* If only he had known it was his beloved Rachel who took them!

RACHEL HIDES THE IDOLS

Laban went first to Jacob's tent, into Leah's tent and into the tent of the two maids but found nothing. After he came out of Leah's tent, he entered Rachel's and with the excuse of the manner of women, she was able to stay seated, perched atop her father's beloved idols. Laban searched the rest of the tent and found nothing. Laban nor Jacob ever questioned Rachel. Why? It was automatically assumed that the pretty, loved one was telling the truth.

How many times had she pulled the *daddy's little girl* card with Laban and gotten away with it? How many times had she batted her eyelashes and gotten her way? No wonder she had a tendency to behave like a spoiled child. She *was* a spoiled child!

The idols were missing, she was bent toward superstition and idolatry which is obvious from earlier behavior and Laban had searched everything and everyone else within Jacob's group. It must have been a silent knowing between the two men. I mean, after all, they both knew this young lady through and through. This was her daddy and the love of her life. And so it was. . . The idols remained in Rachel's possession.

JACOB SAYS-WHAT HAVE I DONE THAT YOU SHOULD SO HOTLY PURSUE ME?

Jacob was angry and rebuked Laban. *Look, Laban, I know I've done things in the past to warrant being chased away to save my life but what have I done to you? Why are you so hotly pursuing me?*

Jacob had not dealt with Laban in a dishonest manner and Laban knew it. He had not taken anything or anyone that did not already belong to him. He hadn't cheated Laban in any way. Laban would never have allowed it if he had tried. So, Jacob couldn't help but wonder why Laban was so hot on his trail. All Jacob wanted to do was return to his home and attempt to make peace with his family. Oh the frustration he must have felt. It seemed he suffered as much when he was trying to do things right. It can be difficult to live down an ugly past but Jacob's response was indicative that true change had begun within Jacob.

Jacob had worked for Laban to acquire what he had. His behavior was above board and his ethics in place. Jacob had dealt honestly with Laban and God had blessed both of their families. Jacob realized this and at this point was not afraid to confront it.

JACOB SAYS – IF GOD HAD NOT BEEN WITH ME – YOU WOULD HAVE SENT ME AWAY EMPTY

What have I done to you to make you chase after me? You have searched my stuff and what have you found. Nothing! I have been with you twenty years and never cheated you. If there was a loss, I bore it, not you. I sweated all day, froze at night and rarely slept. I served you fourteen years for your two daughters and six for the cattle. What have you done? Changed my wages TEN times! If not for the God of my father, the God of Abraham and the fear of Isaac you would have made me leave with none of this! God has seen my affliction. God has seen the labor of my hands and HE was the one that rebuked you last night!

Jacob had finally begun to realize that all his wheeling and dealing and all of his expectation that someone else would take up the slack and provide for him in a crunch was not where he found true success. It was God who had Jacob's back all these years. Jacob had left his home and family. He was alone with family, yet strangers and his cousins were certainly not on his side. His uncle was always trying to figure out how to get over on him. *Don't think I'm not aware Laban, if not for God, you would have sent me away empty handed!*

JACOB AND LABAN MAKE A COVENANT

Laban, of course, being the territorial man he was had a much different view of things. *These are my daughters, my children, my flock! All you see is mine! But what can I do to my daughters or children? So, come and we'll make a covenant.*

So they piled up stones at a place Laban would call Jegar Sahadutha, meaning heap of witness but Jacob would call it Galeed, also meaning the heap of witness. A pillar was set and a promise made that even though no man would be there to see it, neither would ever cross beyond that point to hurt the other.

Even Laban recognized that Jacob was special and that he was going places because it was Laban who initiated that part of the agreement. Why would he do that? He was the one pursuing Jacob. He was the one claiming that Jacob had taken what was rightfully his. For years he had hoped to and even managed to keep Jacob contained and confined to his area but as God would have it, Jacob must return home and continue to grow. How much of that Laban recognized and to what degree it intimidated him is evident in the agreement he insisted Jacob make with him. Jacob, though, had no issue with that agreement. His intent was not to hurt Laban or take from him. After all, he had dealt more fairly with him than anyone else in his life. His only intent was to reconcile his ugly past and make his way home to his family.

It seems Jacob has trouble on both sides. He has essentially burned his bridges with Laban and long ago burned bridges with his family. Either direction he travels at this point is precarious. But God has instructed him to return home and return home, he must. There comes a place of no return, a place where reconciliation beckons and obedience is imperative.

PART 4:

UGLY: THE NEW BEAUTIFUL

CHAPTER 11

It's A Beautiful Life!

JACOB SENDS MESSENGERS BEFORE HIM TO ESAU

AFTER LABAN AND Jacob parted ways, Jacob continued on. As he went on his way, the angels of God met him and when he saw them he said, *"This is the camp of God!"* So Jacob named that place Mahanaim, meaning two armies. It was evident that God was still with Jacob as he promised he would be but facing Esau and coming away alive and well still weighed heavily on his mind.

In hopes of appeasing, Jacob sent messengers ahead to his brother Esau in the land of Seir and told them, *When you see him, this is what you are to say to my master Esau: 'Your servant Jacob says, I have been staying with Laban and have remained there till now. I have cattle and donkeys, sheep and goats, menservants and maidservants. Now I am sending this message to my lord, that I may find favor in your eyes.*

The deployed messengers soon returned with a message of their own. *Your brother is coming and he's bringing four hundred men with him!*

ESAU IS COMING WITH 400 MEN

Now there was no turning back. Esau was on his way and Jacob was less than excited to hear the news. *Everything I fear is about to happen, yet there is no turning back. All that I originally ran from is now inescapable, only now I am responsible for all of this! The animals, the servants, the women and the children!*

Oh, the thoughts racing through Jacob's head as he listened to the news that Esau was on his way with four hundred men. *What did that mean exactly? Why so many?* He *must* be intent on destroying Jacob as he had promised but as large as Jacob's company had become, it would not take four hundred men to kill them. After all this time, did his brother *still* hate him? Esau's intentions were unclear but his excessive company made the dread Jacob felt almost unbearable.

JACOB WAS SO AFRAID HE DIVIDED HIS PEOPLE INTO TWO BANDS

Jacob knew there was a likelihood his days were numbered where his brother was concerned but God had instructed him to return home and return he must. He did the only logical thing he could do. He separated his people into two bands in hopes of saving at least some of them if they were attacked. If nothing else, this might serve to protect Jacob's bloodline. Since Jacob had left with only the clothes on his back, surely Esau would assume the first company he came to was Jacob's entire family. The only decision now is who and what he felt he could sacrifice if need be. Remembering Jacob's tendency toward favoritism in his family, we realize it was not really a difficult decision at all. Or was it?

JACOB CRIES OUT TO GOD-YOU TOLD ME TO!

Gen 32:9 *Oh God! God of my father Abraham and of my father Isaac, the Lord who said to me, 'Return to your country and to your family and I will deal well with you'…. Oh, God!*

Sometimes God tells us to do something that looks like the exact opposite of what we SHOULD do. Like Jacob, we find ourselves afraid the mistakes of our past will come back to destroy us and we are powerless to stop it from occurring. It seems our obedience will be the choice that leads to certain destruction. We are certain of God's instruction to return to that place but why and to what end?

We find ourselves under a false assumption that God's promise to deal well with us means comfort and ease. This is not always the case. God says he will deal well with us but He means according to his definition of well.

GOD, I AM NOT WORTHY

Gen32:10 *"I am not worthy of the least of all the mercies and of all the truth which you have shown. Your servant; for I crossed over this Jordan with my staff, and now I have become two companies."*

Gen 32:10 is the first time Jacob really acknowledges his unworthiness. Suddenly he realizes; in his time away from home he has experienced and enjoyed great blessing. Finding it all threatened Jacob's perspective changes. His prosperity represents responsibility for much and many.

When he left, he had only what he had dishonestly acquired from his rebellious brother, a blessing of a future he could not comprehend from that place in his life. If his brother had anything to do with it, there was no guarantee he would have life. Now, a seemingly unattainable future has begun to unfold like an album before his eyes. He is forced to think of each aspect of it and importance in his future.

When he first crossed the Jordan, he was a man on the run with only a staff. Now he must decide how to split his group into two bands in order to better protect them. What a realization! What a moment of truth!

DELIVER US FROM ESAU!

Oh God, please deliver me from my brother, Esau. For I fear him. I am afraid he will attack me and the mother with the children. The mother with the *children?* That would be LEAH. *For you said, you would treat me well and make my descendants as the sand of the sea which cannot be numbered for multitude.* Reminding God of his promise, Jacob knew that God knew if Esau killed him it was one thing but if he killed the children his bloodline would be cut off.

For a change, Jacob realizes what was really important. *Yes, I have this promise but it will never be realized without the presence of Leah (the ugly woman of process) and the children she has borne me. The mother with the children must be protected and spared in order for the promise to be fulfilled.* Oh, to see the smile that must have come across God's face at that moment of revelation for Jacob. *Yes Jacob, that's what I've been trying to tell you all along.*

A GIFT FOR ESAU-MAYBE HE WILL ACCEPT ME

Jacob spent yet another long and restless night out in the wilderness but this time for a different reason. He lodged there that night and determined to take what came to him as a present for Esau. Two hundred she goats, twenty he goats, two hundred ewes, and twenty rams came. Thirty camels with their colts, forty kine, ten bulls, twenty she asses, and ten foals also came. Jacob would give a good gift to Esau. Perhaps it would serve as a peace offering and his brother's anger would subside enough to let Jacob and his family live.

The next day, as they set out, Jacob instructed his servants to go ahead of him with each drove separated and when they came to Esau and he asked whose they were say, they are your servant Jacob's, a present for you. Tell Esau, *Jacob, thy servant is behind us*.

This is Esau's territory. Although Jacob was the rightful owner of the inheritance, this was no time for a turf battle. Jacob was the younger brother and he was approaching humbly, as a servant, bearing gifts and begging for his life. Maybe, just maybe Esau would accept him.

So many years, so much time had passed. *Was the separation between him and his family not enough penance?* All of Jacob's eggs were in one basket. Either the God who told Jacob to return home would soften his brother's heart toward him and all would be well or it would end in Jacob's death. Either way, Jacob was progressing in obedience to God. Now he must accept whatever happened as consequence rightly bestowed on him by God.

JACOB WRESTLES WITH GOD

Finally, Jacob was ready to cross over. He was ready to rectify his past, gain control of the present and deal with the future, whatever that may be. Jacob had been living with his ugly past, his ugly wife and this whole ugly process for a long time. From this day on, life would be different than he had known for two decades. How he would incorporate old and new and whether that was even possible remained to be seen. Never the less, change was in the air. Jacob recognized it. He had come to a place he knew would change him forever. He had crossed this way before a very different man.

Jacob was not a confrontational man but he was a changed man with much at stake. When he traveled this way before, he had nothing to lose. Whatever happened could only be for the better considering he was running for his life. In the years that followed he had not only found a life for himself but had added wives, children, concubines, servants and animals. Jacob now had much to lose and would soon find himself in an intense wrestling match that would last all night long. Why did it last so long? Jacob was not the Jacob who passed this way before and he had no intention of giving up.

Jacob needed God who met him when he left home to meet him now. He needed God who provided him clothes, food and so much more to carry through with what He promised to do – Bring him home in peace!

Jacob wrestled all night. *I will not let go! I will not give up! I will not let you go unless you bless me! I have come too far! I cannot sit back and watch this whole thing fall apart! God, you said you'd keep me, you said you'd bring me back. Here I am. I need a blessing! If I'm going any further, you will have to step in. You have kept me for the last two decades. I have to know you have my back!*

JACOB CALLED ISRAEL-GOD GIVES NAME CHANGE

Not only did God have Jacob's back and not only did God bless Jacob, God gave Jacob a complete name change.

Gen 32:27-28 NIV says, What is your name? Jacob. He answered. Then the man said, Your name will no longer be Jacob, but Israel because you have struggled with God and with men and have overcome.

Jacob, the one who wrestled with God all night was a different man than Jacob who ran away from home. He had been journeying to find yet another place of ease where he might be looked after. His very name meant heel grabber or he who supplants. He was best known for his lack of initiative. He was known as a deceiver, a liar, someone you could not trust but the Jacob that stood in this place was a different fellow.

Jacob had been both aggressor and victim. In regards to deception, trickery and self-serving practices, he had experienced both sides. As a younger man, he was prone to disingenuous conduct. Later God allowed him to live in a place where he was consistently on the receiving end of that type of behavior at the hand of his uncle Laban. In the process, he had a growing family with an ugly woman; a family far from perfect. Riddled with drama, dysfunction and dissatisfaction, it was exactly the opposite of his nature. It was anything BUT easy!

However, the difficult process Jacob experienced gradually made permanent changes within him. Jacob was no longer Jacob. He was a changed man and God gave him a name that reflected the way God saw him. Truth is it was always the way God saw him because God sees the finished product. Even while he continued to act and respond as Jacob, the lying, self-serving, take the easy way out supplanter. God, saw him as a prince. God saw a powerful prince; one who had struggled with God and man and prevailed. God, saw Israel.

Jacob came out of this wrestling match with a physical manifestation of what had taken place via a torn hamstring. He came out with a verbal manifestation through a relentlessly pursued blessing given to him during the struggle. He also came away with a spiritual manifestation of what had taken place not only there but over the course of several years. He now bore a new name. Jacob would no longer be known for deception and irresponsibility that had labeled his earlier life. Though he still bore a few character flaws and imperfections, he had dealt with Laban honestly and when he had opportunity to come away with more than was rightfully his, he did not.

Jacob's name was now Israel, a prince, one who has power with God and man, one who prevails. I can't help but wonder how much of a prince Jacob felt like at that moment. He was a much older man now. He wondered if his brother still planned to kill him. He suffered a bum hip/thigh in a wrestling match fit for a man a third his age and had lost a whole night's sleep! Jacob was in no physical condition to face a brother who lived simply for an opportunity to kill him.

You and I might have been looking for a good place to hide about that time but not Jacob. Tired, dirty and limping due to the searing pain in his thigh, Jacob likely did not feel very prince like but this he did know; he could and would trust God! God, the only constant in Jacob's life would reveal what was important and see him through.

Somewhere inside Jacob was a glimmer of hope, a burst of strength simply from the knowledge he had seen God. His life was preserved. If he lived through a wrestling match with God, surely God could spare him from death at the hands of an angry, grudge holding brother!

HERE COMES ESAU! FACE TO FACE AGAIN

Here comes Esau. Did fear grip Jacob? Was he determined not to let it show?

As he sees Esau coming, he lines his family up accordingly. The hand-maids and their children were placed in the front, Leah and her children second and Rachel and Joseph bringing up the rear. This line up speaks volumes about who Jacob still desires to protect. Still, he was looking out for his beautiful Rachel and beloved Joseph.

At this point, ugly wife Leah and her children fell in the middle. This actually showed progress in Jacob because his attitude toward Leah for so long stood to earn her a front row seat in the Jacob/Esau drama about to unfold. Still, Rachel and Joseph were most protected, bringing up the rear as Jacob went before them.

This in itself indicated growth in Jacob. No longer hiding behind a woman and expecting her to fix things. Though Leah was certainly strong enough, she wasn't the type to go there and Rachel had proven she simply did not have it in her. She remained reliant on Jacob to step up and make it happen as she demonstrated with attitude toward her early barrenness.

Jacob… Israel… bowed himself seven times as he came near to his brother Esau. God had just told him He recognized him as a prince who prevailed, yet Jacob, when approaching Esau bowed subserviently! Now that IS progress!

ESAU GREETS JACOB WITH KISSING AND CRYING

Much to his surprise, the trauma and drama Jacob expected did not ensue. When Esau saw Jacob he ran toward him yes but only to hug him and fall on his neck kissing him. It was such an emotional reunion that both men wept! Jacob's weeping likely came from a combination of the joy that his brother might accept and forgive him and sheer relief that he was not about to die!

The first thing Esau wanted to know from his brother? *Who are all of these folks?* Breathing a bit easier, Jacob told Esau they were his children and he then brought them forward to bow before Esau one group at a time.

Esau's second question for his brother; what do you mean by all you have sent ahead. Jacob attempts an explanation. *These are to find grace in the sight of my lord.* Esau must have chuckled a bit as he replied, *"I have enough, my brother. Keep what you have for yourself."*

At Jacob's insistence, Esau would accept his brother's gift. Jacob was just so happy to be crying and hugging his brother rather than fighting to the death that any gift he offered was well worth it. After all, he had great acquisition. It must have been amazing to both men; the maturity and love they both demonstrated to each other but at nearly a hundred years old, it's about time they learned to get along, don't you think?!

For us, revisiting the past can be difficult as well. The Word of God has come forth. It's time to return, to re-visit the ugly past, to reconcile, to sift through old memories and heartaches. We can glean from anything that might be useful in forward movement and progression toward the promise.

Suffering a type of post-traumatic stress we find ourselves almost paralyzed; afraid to move forward, afraid to hope again, to dream.

Some situations are so terribly gruesome that it is terrifying to travel back the way you came. To come to a place where everything is a reminder of what you ran away from so long ago. After all, when you ran away, you ran for your life and now you know, and God has said, it's time to return but what if you *die* in the process?!

Still wrestling with who we really are, facing a fearful past and an uncertain future, we fear forging ahead now more than ever. We have always had as much to lose but there was a time it was not always tangible. One might say we are in a sense still protecting the promise in our own strength. All our eggs are carefully laid in this one little basket and we aren't too anxious to place any of them at risk.

But something deep inside . . . the *truth*, says it is imperative you return. Yes, it is absolutely necessary you go back the way you came, at least for a season. If you do not, what good is all you have experienced? What benefit will come from this ugly process if it never comes full circle? How will your promise come to fruition if you do not reconcile with the ugly past.

JACOB STOPPED TO BUILD A HOUSE

For Jacob, all was well. The gift he gave Esau was a drop in the bucket compared to the price for his life! Jacob told Esau, *to see your face is like seeing the face of God, now that you have received me favorably.*

Now Esau is ready for the entire group to head home. *"Let us be on our way; I'll accompany you."* But Jacob declines and insists Esau go ahead. He promises to meet him at Seir and refusing Esau's offer to leave some of his men behind to help, says he only need find favor in the eyes of his brother.

So, Jacob sets out for Seir after Esau's departure but makes the decision to stop at Succoth or the place of tents and build at least semi-permanent dwellings.

You have to wonder why Jacob chose to stop and set up at this place after promising to meet Esau at Seir. Was he simply looking for a good place to rest a while after finding peace with Esau? Was he doing his best to keep a bit of distance between Esau and his people as a precautionary measure? Was it a result of lack of complete trust? Or was it really as he said, he did not want to put stress on the children and the animals.

We are not sure exactly what his motivation for stopping short of all the way home was but it appeared Jacob was still wrestling to some degree with who he really was and how to face this difficult past and uncertain future.

It seems the worst is over. After all, Esau had not killed him at first sight as he had vowed, but this family was known for its trickery. Now Esau is offering to travel with him, offering to leave men behind to help, wanting Jacob to come and join him at Seir. Could Jacob take Esau's words at face value? Could he know for sure? He must have entertained some doubt. Only time would tell.

Jacob was finally ready to settle down for a while. He found his way to the Canaan city of Shechem, bought a piece of ground and pitched his tent. He even built an altar he called El Elohe Israel, meaning God, the God of Israel.

DINAH GOES FOR A WALK

When all was settled, sister Dinah, the last child of Leah and Jacob went out to visit the women of the land. In the process, she met Shechem, the son of the area ruler who took her and violated her. The Bible says his heart was tender toward her and he wanted her for a wife.

When Jacob heard what happened, the boys were in the field so he did not speak of it until they came home. Apparently Schechem's father also heard because he found his way to Jacob to discuss the matter. Hamor explained to Jacob how much his son loved Dinah and wanted to marry her. *We will intermarry, give us your daughters and take our daughters for yourselves. You can settle among us, the land is open. Trade in the land and acquire property. It will be good for both of us.* Schechem would pay whatever price, if only he could have Dinah as his wife.

But Dinah's brothers were furious at what had happened! She had been defiled and they replied deceitfully as they spoke to the two men. They claimed it was important to them that all Hamor's men be circumcised in order for the deal to be made and the two groups to intermarry. Hamor agreed and he and his son made proposal to their people. What they have will be ours, their property, their animals, their daughters. So, every male was circumcised according to the agreement.

Three days later, while they were still recovering, Simeon and Levi attacked the unsuspecting men, killing them all and looting the city where Dinah had been defiled. They also took Dinah back, along with all the women and children of the land and all their possessions.

꒰꒱꒰꒱

Do you ever wonder why we do not see people who rise up against us judged by God for the wrong they have done? It is largely because we have not allowed the process to develop the character in us that would produce the kind of life that allows God to deal with our enemies properly. We remain too eager to see our enemies receive what we have determined to be their due. Though we piously say *"Vengeance is Mine, I will repay, thus saith the Lord"* (Romans 12:19) we inwardly cannot wait to see the settling of the score.

The Bible says we are NOT to rejoice when we see our enemy fall. We are not to allow our heart to be glad because the Lord may see it and be displeased. Until we get this right, we are holding God to the fire and placing him in a position that will not allow Him to bring judgment upon our enemies.

Dinah got into trouble. Sometimes during our process, we get into trouble as well. Dinah though, was not in Schechem behaving like a harlot as some may suppose. If you look at Dinah closely, you will see she was looking for something. Not a man but a woman. Dinah was quite possible attempting to connect or network with someone. Maybe she needed a friend.

In our process, many times with a pure heart, because it is such a lonely walk, we begin to look elsewhere for networking or connections to help get us from here to there. The problem is we become involved in things we should never be involved with.

This is what happened to Dinah. Hamor's son was a prince and the Bible says he loved Dinah. This was something new to Dinah as she had never seen Jacob love her mother. It must have felt warm and fuzzy to Dinah for this prince of Schechem to love her. It was new and exhilarating. This was a new experience and as all young people, she was probably determined to have a different lifestyle that that of her mother. She would not be with a man if he did not love her. Period. Now, not only was she loved but by a prince!

But what we know that Dinah did not is that the enemy of our souls never places something in front of us that is unappealing.

Dinah left home looking form the companionship of women but wound up with something very different. She had only the influence of her mother and aunt's rivalry and there had to be something more. Not only that, she was surrounded by men!

Dinah should have stayed within her surroundings or her people but she did not and it brought trouble. For her innocence or even ignorance, there was a high price paid. The men of Schechem wound up losing their lives and Levi and Simeon paid a price they never thought possible. Jacob would never get over what the two had done. This would be obvious all the way to the time of his death.

Jacob's immediate reaction to the men's behavior; *Simeon and Levi, you have made me a stench among the inhabitants of this land. I am small in number and now they are going to gather together against me and destroy me and my house. Of all the crazy things you could have done. Just when I escaped death at the hands of my brother, you want to go and pull a stunt like this. Now we are in trouble.*

Once again, it's time to go!

CHAPTER 12

A Clean House -
Beauty Control For The Promise

JACOB RETURNS TO BETHEL – CLEANSES HOUSE OF IDOLS

WHAT TO DO now? The children of the ugly wife he never wanted in the first place have now embarrassed and humiliated him beyond measure. Can you imagine what must have gone through Jacob's mind? To be forced out of his home and away from his family, spend years away, finally a chance to come home *and* live only to risk death at the hands of the people of the land because of something the children of the ugly wife! *Does it ever end?*

How many times have you asked yourself that question? When will the embarrassment and humiliation cease? After all, it's not even something you are doing that is bringing on all of this drama.

In Jacob's case, it was his children. In our case, it could be children or it could be any part of the process God is using to perfect us. No matter what it is, it is devastating.

In Jacob's case it was Simeon and Levi that had failed him. Or so he thought. As it would turn out, it was that very same terrible act committed by those impetuous, disobedient, children that would keep anyone at bay who may consider attacking Jacob and his family as they passed through the land. Once again, a part of the process used to further the plan of God in Jacob's life.

When our kids act up, we must keep in mind that it does not negate God's promise to us and covenant with us. God uses it for good. In some way, the worst of trials, especially those we do not bring on ourselves work to support or enforce and thereby give credibility to the Word God has already spoken.

You may perceive it one way, when in fact it may be seen exactly the opposite by others. Jacob's group was so feared after what his boys had done that they found safe passage all the way back to Jacob's homeland. The people of the land were too afraid to attack them after hearing what they had done to Schechem's group.

Who knows what opposition they might have faced if that had not happened before they finished their return. Jacob had refused Esau's help, so he and his men were long gone. Jacob's family was in essence, defenseless. It had been a long time since Jacob had passed that way. Times had changed but God was exactly where he had been all along; with Jacob and all of those children and that ugly wife!

BACK TO BETHEL

God speaks, telling Jacob; go to Bethel, dwell there, make an altar to the God that appeared to you there when you ran for your life. *Remember Him? Remember that time Jacob? Remember when you were alone, with nothing and as much as you thought you knew about me, you hadn't experienced me at all? Remember when your pillow was a rock? Your life was a mess? Your family had turned their back on you? Your choices had all backfired and all your best efforts produced nothing? Do you remember when I met you there Jacob? Go back there. Strip down to nothing Jacob. Remember when I made you that promise? Remember what we agreed upon? I've kept my end of the bargain Jacob. Now, it's time for you to do the same.*

Ahhhhh, suddenly Jacob remembers. *Oh, yes, I know that place. I remember that time. That was a two-part conversation too. God, you made me a promise back then but I made promises as well. As I journey home, safely, with my huge family and abundant possessions, I realize I haven't really kept my end of the bargain. . . but I know just what to do!*

Jacob then tells his entire household to put away the strange gods that are among them, be clean and change their garments. *We are going to God's house. We are going to visit the God who visited me in the day of my distress and was with me everywhere I went. He was there for me when I was completely alone. He brought me to this place and gave me all of you. I promise him if he brought me back, I would do right. It is time to quit playing around.*

You see, Jacob knew things weren't right within his family. He knew his beautiful Rachel was not as perfect as he had hoped. He must have known she was the one who took her father's idols. The idolatry and superstition she dabbled in was evident as far back as the mandrakes that held such importance to her and her hopes of having a child.

Jacob may have been selective in what he chose to believe about beautiful, beloved Rachel but blind-love could only go so far. After all, Rachel was not there in that wilderness between home and Laban's house so long ago. Rachel had proven to cave easily under pressure. She gave her handmaid simply to compete with her sister. She blamed Jacob and pressured him claiming she may die if she couldn't produce a child, when in fact it was childbirth that would eventually take her life. She stole her father's idols knowing it would cause even more trouble between him and Jacob. Jacob had thus far over-looked these characteristics likely because of his great love for Rachel but time had come to clean house.

Jacob says, *let's go!* Jacob's people gave him all the strange gods in their hands and the earrings in their ears and he hid them under the oak by Shechem.

You have to wonder what might have been said or what glances exchanged as the stolen gods of Laban were added to the mix. Everyone had been present when Laban had earlier come looking for his idols.

Either way, it didn't matter now. It was time to put them out of the house. Anything Jacob had inadvertently or overtly tolerated by way of strange gods was being done away with now. It was time to pick a side and Jacob needed that side to be secure. No games with God, this was serious. Those in the land he must travel through were NOT forgiving family. There was little chance of a happy ending simply because they were blood kin and could forgive each other for some long ago family spat!

TERROR OF GOD ON THE CITIES

As it turns out, Jacob's actions proved successful. The Bible says, as they traveled, the terror of God was upon the cities that were around them and they did not pursue the sons of Jacob. Was this because of what Simeon and Levi had done to Shechem's people? Were the surrounding people fearful that the same might be done to them? We don't know for sure what they might have thought but if so, that is a prime example of God working things together for the good of those that love Him. (Romans 8:28)

So Jacob returned to Bethel, the House of God, formerly known as Luz, the place of separation. He and all he embraced and resisted returned to that place right in the middle of Canaan. He and all that were with him returned and as the Lord would have it enjoyed safe passage, exactly as God had told Jacob.

Doing as he was instructed, Jacob built an altar and called the place El-bethel, or the God of Bethel because this was the place God first appeared to him and that same God had brought him here safely once again.

GOD REITERATES JACOB'S CHANGED NAME

After Jacob's return, God appeared to him acknowledged that Jacob's name was and had indeed been Jacob. He was exactly what his name said he was-a deceiver. His thought processes, his choices and his actions were all according to the nature of Jacob. All that had been was true. It happened. And for the most part, it was really quite ugly. The difference now? God is changing that name and Jacob will not only not be *called* Jacob any longer but will not be what he has been in the past; he will not BE Jacob any longer.

Look how far he has come! Look how long he has carried the promise before any significant change manifested. Even when God met him at Bethel and reaffirmed covenant with him, he continued to be Jacob. Even as his life took turns and twists and he began to experience what it feels like to be deceived, he continued to be Jacob. Even as God released him from Laban and reconciled him to his brother and his home country and informed him he would be called by another name, he still was not quite finished being Jacob.

It is now that God says to Jacob, *Look, you are Israel, you can no longer be Jacob because you are Israel.* You shall not be called Jacob any more. You ARE Israel. Be fruitful and multiply. A company of nations shall proceed from you and kings shall come from your body. The land I gave Abraham and Isaac I give to you and your descendants after you.

His name now is Israel, meaning he who prevails with God and man. Jacob has struggled but he has prevailed. Jacob has tugged and pulled and rebelled against God and all He has set forth for Jacob but now, Jacob has at long last began to develop into the promise carrier God had created him to be. FINALLY!

SET UP PILLAR-DRINK OFFERING POURED OIL ON IT

Gen 35:11-12 NIV And God said to him, I am God Almighty; be fruitful and increase in number. A nation and a community of nations will come from you, and kings will come from your body. The land I gave to Abraham and Isaac I also give to you and I will give this land to your descendants after you.

God took the time to reiterate once more the promise given to Abraham and Isaac. Jacob, now Israel could see that God was keeping His end of the bargain and it was time for Jacob to keep his.

Jacob set up a pillar in that place and poured a drink offering on it and poured oil on it as well. Pouring out oil in the Bible symbolizes purity or the Holy Spirit and its influence. Jacob had cleaned up his house and it was obvious God finally had his attention. Jacob's drink offering represented his intention to stop squandering what God had given, cease and change his selfish ways, stop focusing on what he wanted or what he perceived the promise to be. It was time to give God more. He has wasted so much on himself and his own selfish desires.

Our drink offering represents our commitment of service to the Lord as well. Have we come to a place where we stop focusing on self and begin to focus on service to God? When we do, there will be no mistaking it. We will do whatever it takes and make whatever change necessary to align ourselves with the covenant of God.

RACHEL-DIES NAMING BENJAMIN

Though it doesn't seem to be particularly highlighted, Rachel was pregnant with a second child as they journeyed from Bethel. Along the way she began having hard labor. Her midwife assured her that the son she carried she would have but what she did not say was that Rachel would not live through the birth of this child. It was shortly after that Rachel died. As her soul was departing, she named this son Ben-Oni but Jacob who must have been close by his beloved Rachel stepped in renaming the child Benjamin.

True to her nature, Rachel began to fail in her faith as the intense travail, hard labor and near now to death. Her misspeaking mouth was once again prematurely engaged and sadly, those would be her final words. She attempted to name the child Ben-oni which means *son of my sorrow* but oh no... Jacob finally steps up. He has recently had an encounter with God that had brought forth much change. He makes a decision. This sons' name will NOT be Benoni, son of my sorrow. He will be called Benjamin which means *son of my right hand*. Rachel had given birth to son number twelve for Jacob.

As your promise finally begins to present itself for delivery it is not an easy thing. Travail is intense. When we reach this stage we think surely NOW it will smooth out but at this point the promise itself seems as though it is destroyed or dead. No man knows what holding on to this promise has cost you. The maintenance of it, the emotional cost of it, and the pressure it has placed on you.

Rachel's thinking? *All these years you have loved me, cared for me. All I wanted was to give you sons of promise and now, all I produce is sorrow?* She dies with that line of thinking. The promise appears to have failed. Oh no. It is by no means over. Jacob steps in and steps up. I will not allow that name to be placed upon my son. This will not be the child of sorrow. This child will be the child of strength and power. This may be the end of my beautiful, precious promise but it will not be the end of the fruit of that promise!

It is beautiful, interesting observation that while Joseph, meaning increase was born during a transitional time from Jacob to Israel, Benjamin, meaning power, right hand or strength came after the transition was complete. Joseph and all of the children of process were born to Jacob, the supplanter. Benjamin was actually born to Israel, the prevailing prince! Power only came when God said; *you will no longer be that, you are now, this!* Benjamin's arrival one moment before would have been one moment too soon.

What brought Jacob to the place of decision for Benjamin's name; maybe, partially because it was his responsibility in the first place? This was not so in Jacob's household. The children of Jacob were named by their Mothers but this was not the traditional thing to do.

Children in this society were usually named by the Father but Jacob was still going through the process. By nature Jacob left a great deal to others he should have handled himself. It was a pattern in his life. He had been weak and wishy-washy and the only thing that got him up and going originally was his brother's intent to kill him. Then the Lord placed Rachel in front of him and he was so smitten with her and had such desire for her in his heart that he was more than willing to get up and work for her but this was, yet again, an altogether different situation with different motivation.

Jacob was not about to let his promise go out this way; in weakness and death. No, this promise was destined to produce and though the fruit of it still looked small and weak, it would not remain so.

Jacob, now Israel had gone through too much to let the death of his beautiful Rachel stop him. He now realized the actual promise he originally thought hinged on Rachel herself, was bigger than any one of them or any one child borne to him. It was amazing and truly, just beginning!.

THE RIGHT HAND – THE HAND OF POWER

Benjamin was son number twelve. The second son of Rachel and the son of *her* sorrow for she died during his birth. He was the son of Jacob's right hand. He represented the right hand or moving, working hand of God. This right hand refers to the power and the glory of God. Often people use the expression, *this is my right hand man*. People on whom we want to bestow honor are seated at our right hand. World leaders will reserve this position for trusted confidants. Jesus is at the Father's right hand.

In that right hand, there is power and victory. Psalm 98:1 says *"O sing unto the Lord a new song, for He hath done marvelous things. His right hand and his holy arm, hath gotten him the victory."*

Benjamin was the baby in the family but would later be instrumental in helping to joyously reunite a fractured family. Whether out of love for their half-brother or respect for an aging, ailing father the divided group of men, Jacob's sons would be willing to risk their lives for their youngest brother.

What if Benjamin's name had remained Ben-oni? What legacy would he have carried for Jacob then? He helped to bring about restoration and reconciliation of Jacob's children but this might not have been the case if he were named *son of my sorrow* instead.

The possibilities of how Benjamin could have brought sorrow to Jacob are endless. More than one of his sons was the source of much pain and trouble throughout his life. Not so with Benjamin. Jacob would see to it that did not happen. This was the son of his right hand. This was the one who would bring power to all the promise of God. This was the one who would help to bring it all together in the end.

History shows that the land of Benjamin would eventually serve as a buffer zone between Israel and Judah after the division of the kingdom. Powerful leaders such as King Saul, Judge Ehud, Paul and the prophet Jeremiah were Benjamin's descendants. When Jacob delivers his final blessing to his twelve sons in Gen. 49, Benjamin is described as a wolf that prowls, devouring his enemies in the morning and dividing up the spoils in the evening.

What name do you carry? Who gave it to you; your parents, your spouse, your church members, your pastor? Have you demonstrated characteristics of that name in a positive or negative way? It is difficult to realize, you may actually BE that very thing but the good news is that God can and WILL give you a new name, just as God did Jacob and as Jacob did Benjamin. He will cancel out the old name and replace it with a stronger, lasting name complete with characteristics worthy of the name.

Jacob was given a new name. Paul was given a new name. Like Jacob, you may at first be a deceiver that finds himself deserted by everyone but then wind up a prevailing prince. At first you may be directly involved in conflict, you may at some point be used to buffer, cushion, safeguard or shield.

RACHEL DIES AND IS BURIED

Your promise though great and precious will live a short life. In and of itself, it may even appear to die. But *you* will live. The Bible says, except a kernel of wheat fall to the ground and die, it abides alone. (John 12:24). This is true in both the natural and spiritual sense. It will never amount to anything, only what it is. It is beautiful to look upon and foster's great expectation but the beauty of it is fleeting and vain in and of itself. It is about the timing of the promise in relation to the process we must go through and the fruit it ultimately produces.)

The death of your promise is not so much about the promise being unfruitful as it is about your perception of the promise being skewed. If you had been given a choice of enduring all the process had to offer in order to get to what the promise produced, it would not have seemed worth it at the time. *God, had I known what I was about to go through, I would've stayed in a safe place.*

All the promise has produced is all there is to produce. Is it enough? Of course it's enough. It is exactly and completely all that is needed.

Your increase comes (Joseph) and then at the point of death of the promise, power (Benjamin) shows up. That is *all* that is needed. The process has done the rest, laid the ground work, prepared your heart. If increase and power had come before, you would not have been ready.

The truth is; Rachel was gone. The ugly woman Leah long outlived Jacob's beloved Rachel. So will the ugly process in your life long outlive the actual thing you hold in high esteem as *your promise*. But the true promise and its fulfillment is really all about the fruit and *that* is all you need at this juncture. What you perceive to be *the* promise will die but the fruit of it will live and produce beyond anything you can imagine.

Do we see now why the promise itself should not have commanded so much focus and such importance? Can you surmise how Jacob's total and utter devotion to loving Rachel alone was not beneficial to him throughout the process God laid out for Jacob's life? Of course, from our vantage point, it is clear in Jacob's situation. Hopefully, it will now be as clear in our own lives.

ﮞﮞﮞ

The Bible says that JACOB set a pillar upon Rachel's grave. *Jacob, the old nature,* the one who cherished, adored, doted on, pampered, petted, coddled and overprotected Rachel in her barrenness, idolatry and faithless speech. It also says that *Jacob,* set a pillar upon her grave but that it was ISRAEL who journeyed on.

The man who was caught up in the physical beauty of a woman was forced to lay her to rest in a strange place and leave her there. This man must have died inside that day with the overwhelming emotion he felt as he carried her frail body and placed it in the cold, hard ground, but the Bible says it was Israel that continued. The prince of God, the man Jacob had developed into day by day through a grueling, ugly, uncomfortable process would rise from bended knee as Israel and journey on from that grave; a little piece of him, or maybe a big piece, buried there with beautiful Rachel.

Jacob had learned a great deal from that ugly woman he had to live with and guess what? She was still with him. She may have been Ugly, but dependable, Ugly, but strong, Ugly, but productive, Ugly, but producing maturity in a man whose future held greatness and whose past was less than perfect.

REUBEN LAYS WITH FATHER'S CONCUBINE

As Israel carried on, he may have thought his process to be complete and in some sense it was but that did not mean there were not still ugly family issues to deal with.

Just because God changes us and gives us a new nature, doesn't mean everyone around us is on board. It certainly doesn't mean we will not meet with opposition or have trouble; especially when we are dealing with children and even more so, children of process and promise.

Reuben, Jacob's firstborn, the one who held potential for excellence made an imprudent choice to lay with his father's concubine, Bilhah. Seedy news travels fast and it was not long before Israel heard about it.

Reuben, whose mother was Leah, took his half- brother's mother and slept with her. How did Israel hear about it? We do not know but he did. There doesn't seem to be much action taken at this point but the focus was likely taken off Reuben's misstep by the death of his grand-father, Isaac.

JACOB AND ESAU BURIED THEIR FATHER TOGETHER

Gen. 35: 29 says Isaac gave up the ghost and died… and his sons Esau and Jacob buried him. Who would have thought these two brothers would bury their father together without Jacob immediately being killed by Esau? This was a far cry from what Esau had threatened in earlier years.

Instead, after Isaac died, Esau took his family, persons of his house-hold, his cattle, his beasts and all his substance which he had ac-quired in the land of Canaan; and went into the country, the Bible says, from the face of his brother Jacob. He did this because both men had become so prosperous that they had too much between them to stay in the same place; the land could not hold them be-cause they had so many cattle. Jacob though, stayed in the land where his father was a stranger, in the land of Canaan, the land of promise.

JOSEPH, INCREASE - FRUIT OF THE PROMISE

Years would pass and the family grew. It was during this time that the famed story of Joseph takes place. Yes, the same Joseph who finally broke the curse of barrenness on Jacob's beloved Rachel. The cream of the crop! The fruit of the promise! The one everyone knew was the favorite of Jacob-Joseph!

Do you see a pattern here? Are we different than Jacob and Rachel? No, not really. We love the fruit of our promise as well and we love it unconditionally. We will favor, pet, indulge, support, esteem and show partiality to that one small promise, prophetic word, revelation, word of encouragement, word of knowledge God has given us even after he has shown us that is not what it is all about.

Joseph received preferential treatment from Jacob. This angered his ten older brothers. His brothers eventually faked his death to their father Jacob and sold him to a caravan of Ishmaelite traders who were on their way to Egypt.

God gave Joseph the gift of interpreting dreams and when Pharaoh had two disturbing dreams, Joseph was brought before Pharaoh and interpreted his dreams, of seven years of plenty, followed by seven years of famine (Gen 41:8-32). Joseph also suggested how to put this foreknowledge to good use, by storing grain in warehouses. Pharaoh charged Joseph, then at age thirty the rank and authority of a viceroy.

When the famine came, it affected Canaan whereupon Jacob sent all his sons, except for Benjamin, to Egypt to buy food. Joseph broke down upon seeing his brothers (they did not recognize him) gave them food and eventually had his entire family move to Egypt to live.

Jacob's family of seventy people traveled to Egypt at that time and eventually multiplied into a few million before Moses led them out. Joseph had two sons by his Egyptian wife Asenath. The boys were Manasseh and Ephraim. These half Egyptian sons would eventually be taken in by Jacob as his own sons and the younger given the blessing of the firstborn above the older brother.

Joseph's process was more about retaining his worship and his identity in the midst of the most horrible of situations, no matter what happened. All too often our enemy Satan tries to steal our identity, individuality, character, distinctiveness, and our worship, adoration, reverence, respect, devotion to God. This is an on-going spiritual battle with successes and failures throughout the course of our lives. The promise is given, and then the process ensues. Eventually the increase comes but during the grueling, ugly process we cannot lose our identity or our worship!

Joseph had his own promise and process but for Jacob, the beloved Joseph that Jacob thought was lost to wild animals would become instrumental in the further growth and prosperity of Jacob's seed in a foreign land.

CHAPTER 13

Bury Me Next To Ugly!

JACOB CALLED HIS DAYS FEW AND EVIL

AS JACOB STOOD before Pharoah still processing the fact that Joseph, his beloved Joseph is alive and well and more than prosperous, Jacob searches for the right answer.

How old am I? Do you mean in actual years or process? MY days are few and evil; filled with many sorrows. I have been nurtured and protected by the favor and care of God. He has always sustained me through cloudy and sorrowful times but I cannot hold a candle to my fathers in their day. Life has settle now and my process complete. The future? Well, it looks brighter from here. Jacob blessed Pharaoh and went out from his presence.

Jacob was in the land of Egypt with his family for seventeen more years. When he became old and sickly someone told Joseph that Jacob was sick which brought him quickly to his father's bedside and someone told Jacob that Joseph was coming to see him. Even as sick as he was, the thought of seeing Joseph was enough to cause Jacob to sit up in his bed.

Joseph was a busy man, with great responsibility and not much time for visiting his aging father. Joseph though, was Jacob's favorite, as was his mother Rachel and he would always be the fruit, the increase of the promise. There was just something about that promise that continued to impart a supernatural strength to Jacob, even on his deathbed.

Jacob was near the point of death but Joseph's presence was reason enough to muster every ounce of strength he had to visit with him. Besides, there were some very important things he needed to discuss with this son that had been reborn to him.

Jacob had much to tell all of his sons but there was something very important he needed to impart to Joseph's sons as well. Joseph was adored and doted on by his father but he had been taken from Jacob when he was just seventeen years old. God had kept Joseph through many trials but the absence of Joseph from the family made it impossible for Jacob to know what kind of man he had become apart from the obvious.

Joseph's financial increase was immeasurable but it was important to Jacob that Joseph and his sons not forget that they were covenant people. Joseph had not come to find his father when he was free to and this may have caused Jacob to question his devotion or understanding. Jacob's dying exhortation to Joseph's boys was that they not succeed their father in his power and grandeur in Egypt but that they succeed in the inheritance of the promise.

Jacob names Ephraim, the younger first and Manasseh as his sons, just as Reuben and Simeon, the first and second born. The promise was given to Abraham, Isaac, Jacob and now would be continued through Jacob's sons. Joseph, though Jacob's son had missed years of instruction from his father and Jacob needed assurance they would continue as part of the people of God. He appoints each of Joseph's sons as head of a tribe.

How much greater is it to turn from the enticement of worldly wealth and advancement to follow God and faithfully wait for *His* fulfillment in your life. Then again, how much more difficult it can be to make that commitment.

JOSEPH'S SONS-HAND CROSSED BLESSING

Jacob took the time to fill Joseph in on the details of life. He gently laid out a timeline and subtly indicated that his life had been a process. Joseph had been with Jacob when he was young but was so young that Jacob likely never discussed what had happened to his mother or the covenant their family bore.

First he claimed Joseph's sons for himself, placing them under the covenant. Children born to Joseph after Jacob died would be Joseph's to be called after the name of their Egyptian brethren in their inheritance but not so with Manasseh and Ephraim. They belonged to Jacob.

Jacob told Joseph how and where his mother died and was buried then turned his attention to the young men. Noticing the two sons but with eyesight fading, Jacob inquired about them. Joseph told Jacob these were the sons *God* had given him in this place. Jacob's response? *Bring them to me and I will bless them.* After hugging and kissing them, Jacob spoke as Israel, a man who had been through a process. *I thought I'd never see YOUR face again and now God has shown me you children!*

Jacob's eyesight was bad but his mind was clear. He knew how Joseph's sons would be presented for blessing with the eldest on his right but he also knew the command of God. Joseph, thinking Jacob was making a mistake, rebuked his father but Jacob quickly let Joseph know that he KNEW what he was doing. Though they would both become great people, Ephraim, the younger, would be greater than Manasseh.

According to the meaning of their names, just as God gave Jacob the gift in Reuben and the hearing in Simeon, He is giving him more in-crease and the ability to forget the negative past with Manasseh and Ephraim. It was a fresh start in a sense for both Joseph in his difficult yet successful and blessed life and Jacob.

Time was growing short for Jacob. *Joseph, behold I die; but God will be with you and bring you again to the land of your fathers. One more thing Joseph; I have given you one portion above your brothers which I took from the Amorites with my sword and my bow. This one son, I had to fight for, and it is yours.*

‿‿‿

With special attention paid to Joseph, the child of Jacob's beloved promise Rachel, it was now time for a family meeting. Jacob was ready to bless his children. Though his days seemed few and evil to him, he knew they were almost finished and the time had come to gather his sons and speak words of blessing and wisdom and if need be constructive criticism over them.

By now, Jacob had come to identify himself with his new name, his new nature. Jacob was no longer Jacob but Israel. Did his children realize what change had taken place in their father or were they still completely self-absorbed? Unsure of this, we only know that, if they had not, they would soon. *Gather round boys! I want to tell you what's going to happen to you in the last days.* Gather around sons of Jacob, the deceiver and listen to Israel, your father, the prevailing prince with God.

Jacob was a changed man. He was Israel. God knew he was Israel, his family knew he was Israel and most of all HE knew he was Israel but his children were still yet sons of Jacob. They had a process of their own to experience. God had big plans for them and their people and daddy was about to lay it out for them.

Oh, the emotion Jacob must have felt as each name rolled off his lips.

He must have reflected on his stage in life at the time each of them was born. He must have thought of their precious mother Leah. How great were the feelings of guilt and regret he sometimes carried. *If only I had embraced their mother. Though she was ugly and not the one I had chosen for myself, she was exactly what God had chosen for my life. If only I had known how much she would add to my life. If only I could have seen the true beauty she possessed. Embracing her might have bettered the disposition and spiritual life of the beautiful children she produced for me.*

THE GIFT – REUBEN

He first addresses his firstborn, Reuben. *Oh Reuben, you are my firstborn, my might, the beginning of my strength! You were the excellency of dignity and self-respect, and you were the excellency of power and influence, excelling in honor! But Reuben, you are unstable, unpredictable, like water, you must be contained. You went in to my bed, to my couch, to my wife and defiled it. Because of this betrayal Reuben, you will no longer excel.*

Though Reuben was the *gift* and could have produced much with excellence, he was too erratic and his wavering made him unsuitable for this type of distinction. He held firstborn status and a strong name but the betrayal of his father in these latter years was too much to overcome. His actions were enough to disqualify him from the family position he would have held.

His impulsive, unthinkable act of sleeping with his half-brother's mother was clearly punishable by death according to the law. (Lev. 20:11) Reuben only lost his first place status in the family but was fortunate to walk away with his life. His inability to excel and his status lost was a small price to pay compared to what could have been his fate.

Reuben was Jacob's gift but Jacob's gift had betrayed him. Left to our own devices and abilities, our gift will betray us as well. It will uncover our nakedness as Reuben did Jacob exposing us and leaving us vulnerable and defenseless.

Our gift is a mighty, honorable and powerful thing. It can cause us to excel in dignity, honor, self-respect, and give us influence with others but we *must* be aware of its power to lead us to failure as well. If too much emphasis or expectation is placed on the gift, it will fail. If we misuse, abuse or misappropriate the gift it will strip us of not only our dignity but our position, our standing with God.

The truth of the matter is the gift is only a small part of what God has for us. It is a piece of a puzzle. It cannot be ignored, it cannot be given free reign. It is a first step, or beginning of a process including many different facets that will bring us to the place God has prepared for us. We should remember the gift is an instrumental part of the process we must go through but alone is not enough to carry us to fulfillment of the promise.

A false confidence in the gift stands only to highlight its instability. When we are exercising our gift to the fullest and it is working well for us, we are fine with our surroundings but let the water stir and we are shaken to the core. We do not stand strong and steadfast when we rely totally on the gift, no matter where it came from. We can be calm and placid one moment and become a torrential deluge the next. We can be in complete obedience one moment and crossing all boundaries the next. The problem? Any disobedience is complete disobedience. Any wavering in your character, integrity, moral standard, etc. is insubordination to God.

We cannot place our confidence in the gift alone. The gift can and will fail you the moment you rely on it for advancement. The gift can be misplaced, misguided, worn out and wigged out without God's leading and control. Your gift, if not channeled in the right direction, will make you wacky!

Jacob's comparison of Reuben to water was completely accurate. Water is completely unpredictable. It is unreliable, undisciplined and unable to contain itself. Water requires another vessel to hold it in place. It is no surprise that Reuben was characterized this way. He held good qualities and was not openly cruel like his brothers but when he made mistakes they were mammoth in consequence. Confidence must be placed in God just as his father came to realize, Reuben could only be trusted to the degree he was contained. His instability would cost him and his whole family.

If we do not allow God to teach us how to hold our gift in restraint, it will get outside the bounds he has anointed and appointed. We have to discipline ourselves and allow Him to help us keep our gift in check. Instability will take us places we should not go. The gift can also take us places we desire to go but until character is developed within us, the gift itself will not keep us there.

With the gift must come much prayer in order for things to remain in proper perspective. Enjoy the gift God has given you. Use the beautiful, wonderful, precious gift God has given to glorify Him but recognize its weakness, keep it contained in an envelope of the Holy Spirit and conduct yourself accordingly. Remain contained by the Holy Spirit continuously.

THE HEARING, ANOINTING AND INTERCESSION – SIMEON AND LEVI

Gen 49:5-7 NIV Simeon and Levi are brothers—their swords are weapons of violence. Let me not enter their council, let me not join their assembly, for they have killed men in their anger and hamstrung oxen as they pleased. Cursed be their anger, so fierce and their fury, so cruel! I will scatter them in Jacob and disperse them in Israel.

Though similar in disposition Simeon and Levi were completely unlike their father. Jacob was clear. He in no way wanted to be associated with what these two had done. Not then, not now. He was appalled. Though it was many years ago, the bitter taste of this deed was still in Jacob's mouth and the fear of being associated with it on his mind.

Their choice was passionate, revengeful, fierce and uncontrollable. It was excessive to say the least. The swords they used to slaughter innocent people should have been used only for defense.

Jacob was mild-mannered and quiet, not given to over-reaction. Not at all like these two. They were angry and incensed, carrying a chip no-doubt. Their feelings regarding their sister, understandable but the killing of the Shechemites went against everything Jacob believed in. The thought he might die under suspicion of having any part of that was not something Jacob could bear.

Together, Simeon and Levi had done a horrendous thing but they had acted alone. Jacob never forgot. For all he knew, they were the ones who initiated the violence against Joseph.

Therefore, Jacob thought it necessary to separate the two by which their people would be separated and dispersed down the line. This was a way of insuring they did not unite in some reprehensible deed after Jacob's death. Jacob's words spoken over these boys would divide them in their deception and disperse them in prevailing.

Are we aware of the enemy of hearing God? Do we recognize the enemy of the anointing? Anger, self-will, a religious spirit, vengeful thinking or actions work contrary to the anointing. Instruments given us to be used as a defense against a very real enemy are often misused and turned into weapons of offense against others. This is *not* what God intends.

Righteous indignation or anger against things that anger God is understandable and can be a catalyst for helping to right wrongs. This is *not* justification to launch an all-out religious spirited attack against others. If we misuse the tools God gifted us with we become scattered in our thinking. Anger and self-will rise up and threaten to block our hearing and the anointing of the Holy Spirit.

Simeon and Levi are prime examples of being well-intentioned but going overboard. The scattering of their peoples was a terrible consequence. United, properly, they could have been a dynamic duo!

PRAISE – JUDAH

Gen. 49:9-12 says Judah is a lion's whelp; From the prey, my son, you have gone up. He bows down, he lies down as a lion; And as a lion, who shall rouse him? 10The scepter shall not depart from Judah, Nor a lawgiver from between his feet, Until Shiloh comes; And to Him shall be the obedience of the people.11 Binding his donkey to the vine, And his donkey's colt to the choice vine, He washed his garments in wine, and his clothes in the blood of grapes.12 His eyes are darker than wine, And his teeth whiter than milk.

Judah, *you are the one. You* are the one your brothers will praise and bow down to. *You* are the one to subdue your enemies. *You* are the one who will rule as the firstborn.

For us this means praise will carry us. Our praise is what will preach in the end. Not the gift, not the ability to hear, the flow of His anointing, intercession or even works; it's PRAISE!

CONTENTMENT, DWELLING – ZEBULUN

Gen. 49:13Zebulun shall dwell by the haven of the sea; he shall become a haven for ships, And his border shall adjoin Sidon.

We are taught at a young age to reach for, aspire to be, attain, accomplish, achieve. It is not long before that desire to acquire takes over our lives and we find ourselves pawing, scratching and competing in ungodly ways. We compete with family members, co-workers, strangers and even fellow Christians becoming self-centered in our quest. We forget why God gave us a promise in the first place! We are to glorify Him! Sadly, this concept falls by the wayside all too often.

Are you a haven? Do you have a haven? Are you a ship lost at sea with no safe haven of contentment? What about other lost ships? In your contentment with all that God has placed in your life are you a place others can find encouragement, respite? Are you so bitter about the hand you've been dealt that you lost sight of your own lighthouse?

Phillipians 4:11-13 says I have learned to be content whatever the circumstances. I know what it is to be in need and I know what it is to have plenty. I have learned the secret of being content in any and every situation . . . I can do everything through him who gives me strength. This was the ugly woman Leah's position and should be our position as well. Leah realized that even though she could not dictate her relationship with her husband God was on her side. That was sufficient.

And finally, Hebrews 13:5 teaches us to be content with what we have because God has said he will never leave us or forsake us. Contentment, acceptance or sense of satisfaction with our possessions, status or situation, is key to both process and promise.

REWARD, RECOMPENSE – ISSACHAR

The sons of Issachar knew the times. When Jacob blessed this son he was described as a beast of burden who would submit to forced labor.

Gen 49:14-15 Issachar is a strong ass crouching down between two burdens. 15 and he saw that the rest was good and the land that it was pleasant; and bowed his shoulder to bear, and became a servant unto tribute (honor, praise, esteem)

Issachar was a practical man who understood the importance of team-work. Issachar's name is often linked with his brother Zebulun because a willingness to bear burdens brings contentment.

In the song of Deborah, Issachar is mentioned in a favorable light in re-gards to the tribe's battles with the Canaanites. Though slaves or burden bearing people they developed wisdom through it, they stepped up to the plate when it was time to fight and defend.

Maybe they seemed lowly because they were willing to bear burdens but there is a strength and a resolve that comes with the willingness to simply do what needs to be done. The reward is the satisfaction of do-ing what is right.

We develop good things: character, wisdom, knowledge, understanding, integrity, insight, reputation when we have borne the burdens placed in our hearts by God. We can spend our time complaining about the pro-cess and the cumbersome exhausting load we bare, or we can step up to the challenge. God does not allow more to be placed on us than we are able to bear. Sometimes we are simply looking for the wrong things as reward. What God sees as reward (bonus) or recompense (reimburse-ment) for our trouble may be entirely different than what We think.

As we go through the process we learn that there are rewards from God for what we go through. God sees all that we endure and He takes note of everything. Just as Leah persevered and bore the heartache that came through her husband, she would later enjoy sweet reward and recompense from God.

JUDGMENT, VINDICATION – DAN

16 Dan shall judge his people as one of the tribes of Israel 17 Dan shall be a serpent by the way, an adder in the path that biteth the horse heels, so that his rider shall fall backward. 18 I have waited for thy salvation, O Lord.

Dan traveled with Jacob and the family from Padan-Aram to Canaan, and then later to Egypt. When Jacob blessed his sons in the end it is stated that Dan would provide justice for the people.

The tribe of Dan is reprimanded in the song of Deborah for not participating in the war against the Canaanites (Judges 5:17) They failed to conquer the portion of land of Israel that was given them as their original inheritance. That failure forced the tribe to move north and take over another piece of land renaming it Dan (Joshua 19:47). This displacement allowed the people of Dan to find themselves caught up in pagan worship of a golden calf. There would be judgment to come.

This should serve to warn us that fleshly acts and the search for our own vindication is not only unproductive but actually counterproductive leading us away from God's intended path.

Dan would provide a type of justice as one Hebrew meaning suggests but mostly, Dan would contend for his people as another suggests. Compared to a viper along the path, his tribe's conduct would definitely stand out, leave a footprint, or mark but not in the way Rachel had hoped for this lovely child she called her son.

Dan was a fleshly attempt by Rachel to bring for the promise but Jacob had learned a valuable lesson from ugly wife Leah. He had gleaned from the ugly process in the area of vindication. Jacob only had one thing to say. Genesis 49:18 *I have waited for thy salvation* or *I look for your deliverance, O Lord.* Jacob it seems realized that only God could deliver, only God could vindicate, only God would be the judge and that was more than enough.

Is God the one bringing judgment to your situation? Is it God who decides what stands and what falls in your life?

TROOP – GAD

Gen 49:19 Gad, a troop shall overcome him; but he shall overcome at the last.

Make no mistake, there will be attack. During process, promise and all places related, spiritual attack of the enemy will come and will be fierce. For Gad, the Bible says, a troop shall overcome him. Countless times we may feel overwhelmed, outnumbered and overcome as we journey through process into sweet abundance of the promise. We, like Gad, shall overcome at the last!

We are covenant children just as Jacob and his family and we are loved and favored of the Lord. Because of that, the enemy will not prevail. *Psalm 41:1* says *By this I know that thou favourest me, because mine enemy doth not triumph over me.*

It may seem as though we are alone in our troubles. We are not. Though it seems we will and we sometimes feel we are overcome, we will prove overcomers in the end.

When it seems like you are alone, you must realize – you and God alone are a *troop*! The troop we are through the Holy Spirit is more powerful than the troop trying to trample us! Though assault, incident and confrontation seem to be around every corner the *Calvary* is coming! We are not alone! We are a troop!

HAPPINESS – ASHER

Gen 49:20 out of Asher his bread shall be fat and shall yield royal dainties.

When Jacob blesses his twelve sons, he said Asher would have a life blessed with an abundance of food and delicacies befitting a king. Asher would certainly enjoy prosperity and material things.

Ahhh, to be Asher! His name means happiness. He and his people were prosperous and had nice things. It sounds quite comfortable doesn't it? Well-bred and high class, Asher was a child of the ugly woman after all. He is what happens when we continually yield ourselves to the process God has choreographed!

We must remember the tribe of Asher also failed to drive out the inhabitants of Phoenician towns in the area of Israel that they were given as an inheritance. In the Song of Deborah in Judges, Asher is reprimanded for not helping during the fight. Like a big, fat cat Asher sat back, enjoying the good life and was unwilling to step up during war time.

Comfort and well-being are wonderful but we must guard against becoming so comfortable we forget or refuse to follow God's instruction in order to inherit the promise.

STRUGGLE - NAPHTALI

Gen 49:21 Naphtali is a hind let loose; he giveth goodly words.

The struggle for Rachel to bear children is long since over. The struggle for Jacob is over as well.

When Jacob blesses his sons in Gen. 49 he describes Naphtali as a deer that has been set free. Maybe as a child he had an independent spirit but since he received his name before his personality traits were known, it is likely more the symbolism of what Naphtali would be freed from. He was freed from the unnecessary, strenuous, violent struggle against opposition. Could it be that by this time he had finally shown himself to be a part of this eclectic group in his own right? All the struggle and pain he may have represented early on may have driven him to prove himself among his brothers and within this dysfunctional family.

Has your struggle to help bring about the promise caused you to continually attempt to prove yourself? Have you sought to gain approval of family, friends, co-workers, authority figures or mentors in ministry? Striving for acceptance and approval can be an ugly, all-consuming process and all it produces is substandard. Your best efforts within your own strength fall short. Strenuous, even violent efforts against the opposition are not God's way. It is not His best for you.

Opposition comes and we must learn to properly respond. Do not get caught up in pointless, unproductive struggles against flesh and blood when it is a spiritual battle we are engaged in.

Rebekah's children wrestled within her. Rachel wrestled for position within the family. Jacob wrestled with God. We wrestle with unimaginable and unspeakable issues in our lives today but God says our struggle is not against people. *Ephesians 6:12 For we wrestle not against flesh and blood, but against principalities, against powers, against the rulers of the darkness of this world, against spiritual wickedness in high places.*

When the process is complete, we will have learned not to continue struggling with people. According to the blessing spoken over Naphtali, there will be freedom and words of exhortation for others that will come out of our struggles. When we finally learn it is not man we struggle with, we can use our experiences, trials and tribulations to exhort others bringing freedom to their lives.

Early on, Naphtali was the child of competition between the process and the promise. Ultimately, he became a part of Jacob's heritage, a part of the promise and its fulfillment. As long as we feel our struggle is with people and we strive for validation we will not be helpful to others in their process. We must find a place of freedom as Naphtali did. It doesn't matter what others think, feel, want, expect or how they judge us in our standing with God. It only matters that God has made us who we are and for his purpose.

Ultimately, our struggles become a part of the fulfillment of our promise. The Bible tells us all things work together for good. Our kicking and screaming, our competitiveness, our fleshly attitudes will ultimately all come together and round out to become part of the heritage we have in Christ. The hard times, the death experiences, the mistakes and mishaps, all of it.

It is important to note that Jesus began his ministry in Naphtali in the area of Galilee and called his first disciples from its shores (Matt. 4:13-22)

The child Naphtali and the tribe Naphtali both represented struggle. Naphtali's people were independent and free spirited but with great obstacles to overcome. Jesus faced his humanity and overcame the struggle of all time. The disciples struggled with themselves as they attempted to follow Christ's pattern. We struggle in ways that are too numerous to list but if we are willing to accept the process, in the end we will realize freedom and victory.

INCREASE – JOSEPH

Gen 49:22-26 Joseph is a fruitful bough, a fruitful bough by a well; His branches run over the wall.23The archers have bitterly grieved him, shot at him and hated him.24But his bow remained in the strength. And the arms of his hands were made strong By the hands of the Mighty God of Jacob (From there is the Shepherd, the Stone of Israel),25 By the God of your father who will help you, and by the Almighty who will bless you With blessings of heaven above, Blessings of the deep that lies beneath, Blessings of the breasts and of the womb,26The blessings of your father Have excelled the blessings of my ancestors, Up to the utmost bound of the everlasting hills. They shall be on the head of Joseph, And on the crown of the head of him who was separate from his brothers.

Joseph was long awaited for by Jacob and Rachel. He was the beautiful son of promise and was favored. Many Sunday school lessons are of Joseph's special coat of many colors given him by his father.

Genesis 49:22-26 says Joseph was fruitful and far reaching but it also said he was hated and shot at by bitter enemies. Sadly, those enemies were his brothers. Still, he remained strong. Joseph increased, prospered, thrived and flourished! When Joseph was not being kidnapped by brothers who hated him, left to die, sold as a slave or falsely accused, he was succeeding on all fronts! It seemed everything Joseph touched prospered.

Blessings of the deep that lie beneath! The very undercurrent in Joseph's life was of increase, expansion, multiplication and proliferation! From the underbelly to the top of the highest hills shall the blessings be on the head of Joseph, the one who was separate from his brothers.

Oh, the increase! Increase: to become progressively greater and to multiply! Yes, that is ultimately what our human nature is looking for isn't it? We are looking to be bigger, better, stronger and more productive. We like the way it sounds but hearing it is not enough, is it? We are looking for proof! We don't feel as though it is so until we can see it with our eyes, touch it with our hands, watch it grow and flourish. We are not quite sure that the ministry the prophet spoke of is really in store for us without tangible proof. Flip through the pages of Joseph's story and you will see that that tangible increase and prosperity at times even alluded someone as blessed and singled out as Joseph. Though he was ripped from the comfortable position of the favorite son, though he was sold as a slave, accused of raping his boss's lustful wife, thrown into and forgotten in prison yet he was the child of promise. He remained a covenant son of blessing and increase.

Numbers 23:19 says, God is not a man, that he should lie; neither the son of man, that he should repent: hath he said, and shall he not do it? or hath he spoken, and shall he not make it good?

If God says it, it is so. God's Word is indisputable whether or not we believe it to be the truth. Though sometimes we see evidence of it, sometimes we are required to blindly trust. The promise was given to Abraham yet he did not live to see the increase of Jacob that would come through that one long awaited much sought after son of Abraham, Isaac. Still, it transpired.

Be aware! There will be those that hate your blessing, despise your favor and long to decrease your increase. Just as Joseph's brothers hated him, the very aroma of blessing on our lives is reason for some to pull back the arrow in the bow and shoot with full force. Even at your worst, they recognize the anointing of God and His favor on your life and they hate it because they are unwilling to pay the price for that favor and the blessing and increase it brings. The responsibility is too much. The cost is too high and watching you bear up under and even prosper through all the pressure only serves to remind them of their inability to do so. Ultimately, that leads to their failure.

It is important to guard your worship and your identity while learning to embrace the process and maneuver into the promise. With increase and power comes a weighty mantle. You must rely only on God for direction and instruction to be led out of prison and into the palace just as Joseph was!

POWER – BENJAMIN

Gen 49:27-28 Benjamin is a ravenous wolf; In the morning he shall devour the prey, And at night he shall divide the spoil.

Benjamin's name means power and power is an ability to act or produce an effect. *It is possession! It is control! It is authority! It is influence!* And finally, it is a source of *energy!*

Benjamin, the son whose birth took the life of Jacob's beloved Rachel was power. Though it seemed he was the one who ultimately brought death to the promise, he was actually the movement and the might – the get'er done, so to speak! As a tribe, Benjamin could devour prey in the morning and divide the spoil or plunder in the evening. That quick! The fierceness and quickness of progress and production in this people brought about change and served as a buffer for the other tribes.

The turnaround of a situation in our lives can seem almost immediate when power, authority, and influence are in effect. There can be complete reversal, an absolute U-turn in any situation when God's power is evoked. There can be propulsion into our promise and a possession of it as well with the power of God in control, in authority and energizing but this power does not come without completion of the process. This is something it took decades for Jacob to learn but at last, the realization and the reconciliation with the ugly woman had come. The ugly process had done its perfect work.

BURY ME BY LEAH – THE UGLY PROCESS

29Then he charged them and said to them: "I am to be gathered to my people; bury me with my fathers in the cave that is in the field of Ephron the Hittite,30in the cave that is in the field of Mach-pelah, which is before Mamre in the land of Canaan, which Abraham bought with the field of Ephron the Hittite as a possession for a burial place.31There they buried Abraham and Sarah his wife, there they buried Isaac and Rebekah his wife, and there I buried Leah.

At the end of Jacob's life, he brings his children – no longer children, around him to prophesy of their future and pronounce blessings upon them. He drew his feet up under him, signifying the end. As Jacob neared the end he finally saw clearly what was most important. It was then he commanded his children to bury him by the ugly, unwanted Leah.

When all was said and done, Jacob's desire was to be buried by Leah, the ugly process not Rachel, the beautiful promise. He had come to the realization that this ugly woman and the children she produced were truly the most precious gift of all. Though his beautiful, beloved but frail Rachel was the desire of his heart, it was the ugly woman who had never failed him. Leah and her children, though initially hated by Jacob, remained with him long after the promise had passed away.

The fruit of the process would carry on long after Jacob, Rachel and Leah were gone from the earth. They would multiply and carry out the covenant God had established early on. Rachel's children would be instrumental as well. It is an understatement to say Joseph was significant in the fulfillment of the covenant given to Jacob.

In the end, we too will embrace the preciousness of our ugly process. Though our perception of the promise is beautiful and we have labored and suffered for it, it will be the difficult and ugly process we identify with in the end. The ugly, disgusting, process we have long hated is what we wind up wanting to be associated with. What we thought was a horrendous thing – and it was – somehow managed to produce all the tools we needed to propel us into our destiny. It produced the gift, ferried the anointing, fostered hearing, propelled us into praise, wooed us into worship and it seems precious and beautiful from this perspective.

Our promise did come to fruition. It did bear fruit but only in tandem with the process. The promise cannot produce independently of the process. Like Jacob, it is only through the process that we learn how truly unstable the promise really is.

What the process has produced has cost us the most and what we pay so dearly for we are not as likely to take lightly or disregard as insignificant.

As Jacob learned over the course of decades, our confidence must be in God and His direction for our good and His Glory! Only then, does increase come. As these things are in place we then begin to realize what the promise really is. With this revelation comes power to walk in integrity, honorable character and freedom.

Where do we stand regarding our promise? Well, increase and power continue forever but now, it will do so through the fruit it bore and without the pressure and high maintenance it initially required.

FOREVER IDENTIFIED WITH

It would seem Jacob's dying wish would be to be buried by his precious, beautiful Rachel. After all, for years and years, she was all he could think about. He dreamed, longed, waited and worked for her and when he finally acquired her, he doted on and protected her until the end of her life.

In biblical times, where and with whom you were buried held great importance. It would seem that Rachel would be where Jacob's identity would lie but it was not. Maybe it is better to say that Jacob's identity *was* wrapped up in Rachel, the beautiful representation of God's promise that Jacob chose but Israel was better identified by the, not so pretty princess of the process God has chosen for him, the ugly wife Leah.

Israel's outlook was much different than Jacob's. Therefore it was Israel who made the decision to be buried with Leah. In the end, he realized how truly precious Leah was. Could it be she had become even somewhat beautiful to Jacob? He realized that although he had completely focused on Rachel for the better part of all their lives together, it was Leah, ugly, undesirable, Leah that had helped him become the productive, covenant fulfilling man he found himself to be. It was Leah who gave him the most children. Leah, not Rachel placed less pressure on him in marriage and parenthood. Leah enjoyed longevity and Rachel was short lived. Leah, was the lasting beauty!

It is the process that shapes us as well. After experiencing the process, our outlook is different as was Israel's. When all is said and done and we have been through the long, grueling process, we realize how truly valuable it is. It is the fruit of that process that causes us to realize how very precious that ugly thing was, even when we refused to accept it.

It was that ugly process that gave Jacob the name, respect and notoriety. It was the ugly wife that bore the fruit that supported the limited and fragile pieces of the promise. Without that support, Jacob would not have become what God said he would be. Initially, left up to Jacob, what he thought would bring forth the promise would have died early having produced nothing.

Our loyalty will be as Israel's - with the process in the end, not the promise, no matter how beautiful. Any actual growth we experience comes from the process and the promise will never be productive and powerful without its presence.

Remember Joseph? He was the fruit of Jacob's promise. Joseph would go on to preserve not only Egypt but the Nation of Israel in time of famine. Beautiful Rachel that Jacob so desired was long gone but her son Joseph as hard pressed and cast off as he seemed to be, continued to produce. Yet it was through the ugly woman and her decision to build a foundation of praise, Judah that Jesus would come and save the world!

When our ideal and expectation of our beautiful promise are long gone, the fruit of it will continue to produce good things. God promised us this much but the fruit of our process is never ending. The harvest we gain through living with the ugly woman pays dividends throughout eternity!

CPSIA information can be obtained at www.ICGtesting.com
Printed in the USA
LVOW060526140312

273005LV00002B/2/P